QUOTES BY GREAT PEOPLE

I am in the business of helping people transform their lives. It takes time, effort, and a real passion for a person to change the trajectory of their lives. Every once in a while you come across an outlier, an individual who despite struggling in their previous life, seems to pick up the inertia and is ready to play the game of life at a different level than most. Doug Wood is such an individual. I have witnessed his wholesale growth in multiple areas simultaneously as he sets a new standard of what is possible in self-improvement. It's fun to watch his development as he breaks the shackles of his past reality and now explores every facet of how he can get better. Serve more. Be more. Watch out world; he is becoming a force to be reckoned with!

Dr. Wayne Scott Anderson
New York Times Bestselling Author

We all hear three voices: our self-sabotaging internal dialogue, our true voice, and God's voice. Doug has courageously taken the journey from being imprisoned by his self-sabotaging and limiting beliefs to embracing and magnifying his true voice. He is real, genuine, and authentic, living fully in his gifting and bringing his natural genius to the service of others. Listen closely to what he has to say. It is time to stop robbing yourself and others of your gifts. The world is waiting for you and Doug wants more than anything to show you how to begin this exciting journey.

Dave Blanchard
Founder and CEO, Blanchard Leadership
Creator of the *Habit Finder Profile and Coaching Program*
Author of *Today I Begin a New Life*, *The Observer's Chair*,
and *Equanimity—Conquering Mt. Entrepreneur*

As a pastor and someone raised in The Church, I am always looking for people who are on the same frequency with the Word of God and myself. Someone who is not afraid to confront misguided cultural and personal ideologies. Doug Wood is just that person I was looking for in my life. He is not afraid to speak transformational truth yet wrap it in a heart of love! Allow yourself to hear his heart and wisdom in Church Boy To Millionaire.

Dr. Scott S. Schatzline
Daystar Church
Tuscaloosa, Al

There are very few voices that have so radically helped shift my mindset, business, and vision like that of Douglas Wood. My wife and I have had the honor of sitting with him in leadership and experiencing next-level growth from his knowledge and wisdom. Doug is not only my business mentor/coach, but he is my dear friend. Most importantly, he is authentic in every aspect of his life. The barometer of a man's character is seen greatest behind the front door of his home. Doug's family is a beautiful representation of some-one who has made it his life's goal to guard what matters and at the same time to better humanity. Doug is the coaches' coach! Prepare yourself for radical growth as you read Doug's new book! This book will be gasoline to your goals and vision.

Pat Schatzline
International Christian Speaker, Author and CEO
www.RaiseTheRemnant.com

Doug leads with his heart. He is able to develop leaders and serve at an extraordinary level. He is authentic and empathetic with business savvy that has made him a standout in his field. His zeal for life and passion to change the world has only increased since the day I met him. Now coupled with experience and wisdom this guy is unstoppable.

Jen Jones
Author, Speaker, and Coach
www.JenJonesDirect.com

If you want real, unplugged content that will challenge, awaken, and drive every ounce of potential that you have within you, this book is for you and Doug Wood is your man. This book is for the people that know they have something greater inside of them, even if it's just a small spark of an idea. It's for all the people that want to be more, grow more, help more, and challenge the status quo of this world and elevate to true greatness. In a world that's full of people playing small and giving untested advice, Doug gives you the real message from someone who really has done the work.

Brad Miller
Entrepreneur

Doug Wood is one of the most authentic and genuine people I know. He's not afraid to speak the truth in love to help others move past their concepts and into their greatness. He is a friend, mentor, leader, thought-provoker, and catalyst for helping others become the best version of themselves. His influence on me has changed my life and my family for generations. Beyond grateful to know this world-changer!

Dan Valentine
Entrepreneur and Speaker

Doug Wood is a professional believer in people. He has a profoundly unique ability to challenge the status quo. I've known a lot of influencers in my life that have helped shape me into the man I am today. Doug is at the top of the list.

Corey Baker
Entrepreneur and Speaker
Author of *Chasing Better*
www.CoreyBaker.us

CHURCH BOY TO
MILLIONAIRE

How to Find Personal Freedom and Liberate Your
Millionaire Mindset for Massive Impact

DOUG WOOD

Published by Aradaya
Copyright © 2019 by Doug Wood
All rights reserved

ISBN Hardcover: 978-0-578-47000-9
ISBN Ebook: 978-0-578-47001-6

First published in the United States of America by Aradaya
Printed in the United States of America

www.ChurchBoyToMillionaire.com
www.TheRealDougWood.com

Photography: LaRae Siliga
Cover Design: Ashton Hauff

TABLE OF CONTENTS

A First Look at Church Boy to Millionaire

GREATEST HITS 289

Doug goes completely unplugged with daily-doses of motivational mindsets, actions, and challenges. They're here to help you live your best life.

DEDICATION

This book is dedicated to my daughter Katelyn (12), my son Phoenix (2), and my daughter Amaya (14).

I want each of you to know that when we took off on the plane for Singapore just eight weeks ago, I had a panicked moment that I did not share with you. I thought to myself that if something was to happen to me at this point in my life, not writing this book for you would be my only regret. I have raised you to know God, take personal responsibility, manage your emotions well, create the lives you want, and to have an entrepreneur's mindset. And we have many conversations about each of those—but that's just it, conversations.

I wanted to document, and make sure each of you know my thoughts, how it all started, and what you can be prepared for, as well as exactly what your mom and I have contended for in our marriage, faith, finances, and creating the life we live today. This life has come from God, hard decisions we have made, and the hard work we have chosen to put in, always using you three as our WHY, and never our excuse.

You see, our life didn't always look the way it does now. Amaya and Kate, I know you remember some of it, but there is a lot you don't know. I wanted to leave this for you girls and Phoenix. Consider this a manuscript of where our family was before you were born and when you were younger. It contains the key decisions we've made, the sacrifices we've made, and the mindsets we've adopted and lived by to create the best life we can live, and to become the integrated family we are today.

This book is also dedicated to my beautiful wife, Thea.

Thea, it is because of you that we are where we are, and I get to write this book. Had I said no to you, to coaching, to giving the $12,000, to the house on the hill, or to Phoenix (just to name a few), I know for a fact our life would look much different. Thea, you have contended and never stopped praying for me and this family, even though I wanted to quit during the many hard times. You always see and find the best in me and give me space to do what I love, so I can be my most authentic self. You encourage me and don't let me quit.

Thanks for pioneering our family to never settle, to never play small, but to always dream big. You are the love of my life and the most amazing mother to the girls and Phoenix. This book is for our family tree and for the one person who needs a miracle in their mindset, family, faith, and finances.

HELLO WORLD CHANGERS!

Hello, our fellow World Changers!

When I think about you all cracking open this book, my heart is filled with so much gratitude. Doug has poured his heart and soul into writing out the formula of how we revolutionized our family to live an integrated life. I believe with all my heart, that as you apply the mindsets and action steps throughout this book, your life will be transformed, which will have a ripple effect of abundance and health in your family bloodline.

Doug is my Loverboy and he has given me the gift of being a mom to our three children Amaya, Katelyn, and Phoenix. The girls call him Papa, and our son, Phoenix, calls him Daddy 😊. They seriously love and adore him. We are coming up on nineteen years of marriage. It's been a journey filled with obstacles, choices with which to contend, and a whole lot of breakthrough and adventure.

As a family, in 2018 we traveled two-and-a-half months out of the year. Traveling with a toddler is an adventure in and of itself. We traveled literally all over the world, from the UK to Israel to Croatia to Austria to Singapore and Bali, to name a few.

As we traveled, I had moments when I would look at Doug and watch him ponder. One of the times we were on a beautiful boat looking out over the Amalfi Coast, and I asked what was on his mind. He expressed how awesome it was to experience this beauty of the world as a family. His only wish was that our friends could be with us.

Time and resources were the only thing holding our friends up from having the freedom to travel with us as well. We made the decision seven years ago we were going to be where we wanted to be, or God called us to be, not where a job or extended family said we needed to be. You could see a fire more than ever in Doug, and he knew it was time to write this book, to help empower you to take personal responsibility, to create the life you want, and fulfill the dreams within you.

Doug is for the average person with an above-average desire for more. The reason "why" is because he was in many of your shoes, and he has made it his life's mission to help people break through with the "how to." It all starts with a decision. He made the fundamental decision to take responsibility for his life, his family, and future generations.

He invites you on the journey to discover how abundance and breakthrough starts in the mind. He welcomes you into his personal journey of contending with his beasts, while giving you the tools and mindsets he implemented, to create a life of purpose and fulfillment. His passion is to help you awaken your unique ability and shift your mindset to one of abundance and a life filled with purpose.

Doug gives you the roadmap to take down the beasts robbing you of financial freedom and fullness of life. He is unapologetic in his approach and he comes to you with complete authenticity. I believe, with all my heart, this book is coming forth at the right time for the right people—those who are ready to become intentional parents, intimate partners, and chain breakers for their families. Collectively, we are choosing to shift the tide, empowering all generations to rise up and take personal responsibility, while daily grabbing hold of the tools and resources to live in our unique abilities and fulfill our purpose.

You are going to get to know Doug and our family quickly as you dive into these pages. He is open, honest, and shares with authenticity. He will make you laugh throughout as well. The goal is that you would be awakened with how you, too, can become a millionaire. May you implement these tools, create resources, and bring solutions to the world. The world is a beautiful place. We invite you to Kick Fear In The Face, and take action against the one thing that is holding you up from a Breakthrough Life.

Thea Wood
The Millionaire's Wife 😊
Founder of Kick Fear In the Face,
www.KickFearInTheFace.com
Entrepreneur

PASTOR'S BLESSING

It's one thing to impact a moment. It's another to make someone's day. But to change someone's future? That's an entirely different thing.

That's the kind of impact Doug Wood had on me. As a religious leader, I've had the privilege to connect with thousands of people as a pastor, a chaplain, and community advocate in Miami, Florida. Yet that night in Costa Rica, when I personally met Doug Wood, something about him stood out as a man, husband, father, and entrepreneur. My immediate thought was that we had a lot in common. Little did I know our similar interest in business and ministry would prove me right.

His experience as someone raised in the Church immediately caught my attention, as I remember being that guy. I grew up knowing my purpose was to pastor and lead in the Church, and I have had the pleasure of doing just that for the last 34 years. But back in the day, I was the last one others would see as qualified. And that motivated me to prove them wrong. When I heard Doug's story, dropping out of ministry training as a young man, my mind raced back to how he would have handled all of that. Navigating through thoughts like, "God, am I called to this?" and, "What now?" Anyone who felt the call of ministry would have wondered what to do with it at this point. And yet, when you look at him today, you would never smell the smoke of adversity. No limp. Total security. No regrets. Somehow, he had managed to see he wouldn't fit the mold of the so called "perfect ministry guy." And he was okay with that, and that impressed me. He proved a minister doesn't have a single mold. That's not all of who he his. He is

Doug Wood, a man with a ministry calling and a desire to help people, but he just wasn't going to do it in the typical fashion. He was being prepared for a different kind of platform.

As he shared his story, it was clear his message resonated with everyone in the room. He dominated the platform like any pastor would, as thousands were dialed in to his every word. I'm looking around at the convention crowd full of the sharpest people to grace the earth, and I'm hearing the scurry of pens hitting paper as everyone rushed to write down everything he was saying, everything they were thinking, and every new desire filling their hearts as he spoke to their future. He had articulated every thought and projected them on these massive screens, and it was funny to watch the crowd take breaks from their incessant note-taking to snap a picture of each slide. Before long, I'm finding myself being challenged to stretch beyond where I have been living. In this moment, I'm not the leader, or the speaker. I'm just another face in the crowd. And Doug Wood was showing this face that there's more to my life than what I had been living. I was living a good life, but now I was wanting a great life. No vulgarity. No emotional hype. No flash. This guy was dropping truth bomb after truth bomb, and they were landing in the heart of each and every one of us. I left that place a different man, and I have Doug to thank for much of that.

Where so many in our day have taken on the attitude of play now and work later, Doug has mastered the opposite. He's navigated through the shattered broken glass of setbacks and allowed his faith to be the crucible to build his character and influence. His faith wasn't a crutch, but Doug has found a unique way of balancing the church and business world. He's a new kind of vanguard leader impacting culture and inspiring us to realize good is never good enough. And God has so much more in store.

I once heard it said that the depth of one's ministry is determined by the waters he had to wade through to get there. Whether he's in front of the crowd teaching, behind a computer training, sitting in a room with top level leaders, or around a dinner table with family and friends, you would be quick to realize the impact Doug Wood has on everyone with whom he comes in contact. Doug's words will get everyone to a place where *they decide* to never let anything keep them from their own story of greatness.

Steve Alessi
Pastor, Metro Life Church
www.MetroLifeChurch.com

FOREWORD

I have coached and worked with many people over the last thirty years, from legendary CEOs and visionary entrepreneurs, to leaders in conscious capitalism, educational reformers, and movement makers. It's been a privilege and honor to be part of so many conversations and strategies that are transforming our lives and shaping the future of generations to come. I've enjoyed working with Doug and appreciate the authenticity and ambition he brings to any conversation.

I admire anyone who opens up and reveals what it has taken them to liberate the authentic leader within and share the real journey, beyond the Instagram version we are used to experiencing. Doug has written this book from the heart with his signature straightforward style that I believe is needed today.

What are we trading our life energy for? Knowing the answer to this question is a gift I wish Doug's story reveals to you. Thank you, Doug, for sharing your real story. And to you the reader, I wish that you connect to what this means to you as you turn each and every page.

There are books that are interesting to read, and then there are books that get each of us interested in the meaning of our lives. What you hold in your hand or are listening to right now is a heartfelt gift to each of us from someone who is willing to let their life be a teacher and guide. All any of us can do is lead the life we are called to live and become more of who we know we can be.

Let *Church Boy To Millionaire* be one of those significant influences along the way to make this possible for you. Thank you, Doug, for being who you are and for sharing this gift with the world. The world is eagerly awaiting for all of us to follow your lead.

Helen Urwin
Founder of Bayleon

KNUCKLE BUMPS 👊

Phil Mickelson: Thank you for most likely never getting my letter. And even if it did reach you, and you would have responded and bailed me out, I would have been robbed of the process and this book would not have been written 🏌️👊.

John C. Maxwell: The *5 Levels of Leadership* unlocked the code for me to start this process. It confirmed many things of why old forms of leadership are broken and won't work any longer. I respect you, my friend. Thanks for leading the way 📕👊.

Casey Mitzel: I know for a fact that God chose you to ask me the right question on the day before I would have said NO, and made a huge mistake, possibly costing me my marriage, my ministry, and the miracle of life. I have my son, Phoenix, because you were willing to ask me a few questions and just listen. Thank you. I know Thea thanks you, and I know Phoenix will eventually thank you, too 💪👊.

Helen Urwin: Anytime you get around Helen Urwin and the Bayleon team, your clarity, productivity, passion, execution, and income goes up. Helen, Jess, and Patrick, I can't say THANK YOU enough for making this possible 🖤👊.

Dr A.: There is no other man with bigger vision and heart to serve humanity. Thank you for pioneering HOPE and what HEALTH will look like for me and so many other families. Lori, we lost you too early. But you were the beacon of light to me who modeled love and genuine heart to serve others to me. I miss you and our special talks 🖤👊.

Mike and Sumer Morenz: You came into Thea's and my lives at the perfect time. Who knew that Thea picking you and Sumer up in wine country would turn into being some of the safest, most fun, and purest friendships when we needed them most. I respect you guys so much for contending like you have. We love you and our quality time we spend together.

Karisa Lara: Your friendship is priceless to me. You stand for excellence. You are such a warrior and I'm honored to call you a friend. You challenge me and so many others to rise above the noise and circumstances, no matter what may be going on in life, and make a difference. Thea and I love you and Michael very much.

Eric Hunsberger: Thanks for allowing me to be me. Thanks for being a friend and living in spontaneity with me, for picking up and flying across the country at a moment's notice just because we can. I love our times together and the encouragement you bring.

Kale Buyer: Thank you for being there for a struggling dad, husband, and businessman, for a guy about to burn out, who hid a dying spirit behind a facade and fake smile. You guided me to health and to the right people who put me on the right path. THANK YOU!

Corey Baker: You made a decision, wrote your book, challenged me, and showed what's possible when one makes a decision and commits. Congrats on *Chasing Better* and thanks for being a great friend 👊🍻.

John Santiago: You are the brother I never had. Thank you for being YOU. Golf, laughs, deep talks, bull 💩ing, safe place, free to be me, judgefree zone, and above all, consistent. You make my life better ⛳🍻.

Dan Valentine: You model intentionality, commitment, drive, and no excuses with passion. Thanks for your friendship, leadership, and the example you set for me and so many others 💪🍻.

David and Terri Miller: You stretched me, you challenged me to be open, to never judge, to think differently, to never make assumptions. You are mentors, friends, partners, and of course, the best people to grab a late night beverage with 🥂🍺.

Greg and Roxane Hickman: Loyalty is who you are. You are also my pastors, my friends, dedicated to my children, and have always given me pure love and support without judgement when I needed it most. Roxy, your passionate words of encouragement telling me to GO FOR IT have encouraged me most. Love you both 🖤🍺.

Dad: Thank you for the best start a son could ask for. Years ago you got me in the game early, skinned my knees, and set me on the path of pursuing my dreams as far as I can. I'm still going ⛳🍺.

Junior Siliga: When I was at my first fork in the road at nineteen, God used YOU to make a call I couldn't say no to. You have been a mentor and friend ever since. Thank you for always pointing me to Jesus and the Siliga family friendship.

Brad Miller: You know why you used to drive a 3 series right? And yes, I drove Armadas in my dreams. But above all the nonsense we give each other 💩, you have been a friend. A loyal friend. Thank you for being CONSISTENT in my life and for being the man of character that you are. I have loved traveling the world with you. More to come, cheers.

Dan Hunt: I first met you at a pivotal point in my life when we were just kids ☺. Even though time and life goes by, you have been a friend and like-minded confidant for so long. Thanks for your consistency and the man of excellence that you are. You have made my life so much better.

Steven Furtik: Thanks for leading from the front in your health, passion, and being unapologetic with your message. You are giving the best representation of what the future of relevance in ministry looks like.

Steve Alessi: You are in my TRUTH corner and I value YOU. Thank you for your consistency and your boldness. You are a great man of excellence and a leader to many. When I think of how to show honor and what respect is, I think of you.

Judah Smith: For years, I have watched and respected you and your genuine love for people. Recently, you revolutionized ministry with current technology in launching the biggest and most relevant church plant ever. Going online, challenging the status quo, and showing the church of the future. Well done, man 💻 👏.

Bekah Tinter: I value YOU and our friendship so much. Thanks for making me better. Our voice texts, chuckles, deep talks, and your genuine desire to see families be integrated and together is so pure. Your impact and Kevin's impact on humanity is amazing to watch. Thanks for being a friend to me 🙏 👏.

Mom: I am your son. Starting with my shoe and clothing addiction it's pretty obvious. You raised me well and shaped me into who I have become. You always pointed me to Jesus and never stopped praying. I love these last few years here in Arizona. You have given Thea and I such peace when we travel, knowing that the girls and Phoenix are safe.

Wes Holt: A friend, an uncle, a financial adviser, and a man of prayer when I need it the most. Thanks to you and Paula for always seeing my unique ability, even long before I did, and speaking it to me. You always said, "Doug you need to be with the people and the people need to be with you." Thanks for your encouragement to step out 🙏🧍👏.

Dave Blanchard: Thanks for preparing me well for where things are now. You were right on with some things you said to me that were hard to hear. They didn't make sense then, but they do now. Thea and I needed it most, and it saved us.

Jen Patera: There is no one, and I mean no one, that has shown more grit, will fight for me harder, and always has my back. You have also fought hard for your girls and the person you have become today. I could not be more proud to be your brother and navigate life together. Proud of you.

Jen Jones: Jen Jones Direct! I think everyone needs a JJD in their life. You are someone who has challenged me to be a better leader and to think differently about any situation. You are thought-provoking, fun, joyful, and show others what it's like to live life in the "and" while wearing many hats and serving people with excellence. Thank you for your trust and friendship.

GG: You have loved me unconditionally for forty years. You have always been my biggest cheerleader. Grandma, thank you, for passing on what loving people look like, God's anointing, a life of prayer, and what's possible when one pursues their passion and finds joy in everything they do. I love you, Grandma ♥.

Grandpa Williams: Your love and sacrifice for me, and setting up our family tree to win, has had no end. You taking me to Israel when I was thirteen, and setting my foundation, shaped me. Your prayers, encouragement, honest talks, and no-compromise way-of-life modeled abundance.

Grandpa Wood: I know it's been twenty years since we lost you. I still think of you often. But, a few pew people, even to this day, tell me I remind them of you. A few even ask if I'm a pastor. I stopped fighting and answer the same now, "Yes, I am, but probably not like you think." It just looks different in this generation. Thanks for passing the torch. I promise I will do everything I can to carry it well and serve others 🔥 📖.

Grant Cardone: Thanks for teaching me it's OK to promote myself and what I am passionate about. Your daily videos mentored me everyday for five years and made this possible.

Andy Frisela: Your passion and authenticity inspire me. And you're one of the most REAL dudes I know. You say it like it is and have given me the courage to be me without apologizing for it. You are a key part of this. MFCEO project helps people win at life. Thank you!

Ed Mylett: Your talk at 10x in 2018 was a turning point. You spelled it out. Yes, we are all in a crisis every single day to become the best father, spouse, and person we can be. Thanks for being authentic and showing what most people won't. Your passion and genuine heart to serve impacts my, and I know others', life. Your podcasts are life-giving.

Dan Bell: You taught me to change the way I look at things so the things I look at change. Thanks for removing my negative mindset about money. Your talks and mentorship gave me permission to think differently, understand it's OK to make money, and make an impact.

Heather Oltean: Thank you for loving my wife—especially when you were the only one she could confide in while I was confronting my beasts. You have been a safe place for her and us. Your family's friendship and the strong woman that you are has made a huge impact our life and those around you. The Wood family loves the Oltean family. Friends for life.

Nick Johnson: There is not a more level-headed and poised person I know who listens to truly understand and not just respond, and then always gives such a unique way to look at things. Thanks for your mentorship and guidance in my life and so many areas.

Coach Michael Burt: I now get it . . . Thanks for giving me time, a chance, and showing me what is possible long before I saw it, your persistence to become excellent, and showing me and others that EVERYONE needs a coach in life. You coached me well and I respect you so much for staying TRUE to who YOU are. You are the OG MONSTER!

Eric White: Thanks for coming into my life this year. You are such an encourager and have a way of making someone feel that they can do anything. Thanks for the nudges and challenging me in many ways. I consider you a great friend 😄👊.

Bob Proctor: Thank you for introducing me to Frequency and that this book was already created. I just had to get in harmony with it. My life went to a whole new level at Paradigm Shift and this book went into action that weekend 🏆👊.

Dave Ramsey: Financial Peace University got us started on the path to becoming debt-free. Thank you for being so bold and blunt and telling me exactly what I needed to hear. You challenged me to commit to what's important, and it started with you telling me to increase my income and stop spending so much. Your material changed my life and so many others'. You are a key part of this book! Thank you!

Angie Taylor: Thank for reaching out and pursuing this relationship. Boldness takes courage and you are a woman of courage. We WILL reimagine education and YOUR dream will come true as Valor Global Online will transform and impact humanity in a way far bigger than we could ever see it. Thanks for being a great partner.

Jordan Loftis: This book would not be anything that it is or even published right now if it wasn't for you. You crawled up into this crazy brain, helped me stay in the zone, and truly pulled this book out of me. And in the process, I found a friend. Thank you 👊🙏.

Steve Long-Son/Bogey — ☺ I am so glad you came into my life. You are a brother like no other. Your genuine joy is, and was, so healthy in my life when I needed it the most. Thanks for always having my back!

Dave and Brooke Ross — Thank you for being persistent in asking us to come and speak at your church. It forced me to Kick Fear In The Face and step into something I was resisting. God used you to heal something in me, and you guys are largely responsible for this. Thank you 🙏.

Tom, Jaci, Mandy, Ronnie, Misty, and Tessa — Thank you for trusting me with Thea and bringing me into your family, and for coming into mine. We are better together and I value each of you in my life.

Benny Perez — Your timely message at Breakthrough Conference 2007 changed our lives. That night, generations of lack mindset, poverty mindset, and debt were snapped off of my family. Thank you for being faithful and allowing God to speak through you.

WARNING

Reading this book will come with a few side effects: you will get CLARITY on your PURPOSE, get in better alignment with your spouse, focus on your goals, your income will most likely go up 💰, your health will probably improve 💪, and overall, your life will drastically change for the better.

However, I'm going to say this right up front. This book is NOT for everyone! You might have to eat the fish and spit out the bones. Honestly, if your life is good, you are clear on your purpose, you are happy, you make all the money you want, you love everything about your church relationships and community groups, your family is perfect, and you enjoy your annual two-week vacations, then frankly, this book is not for you. But, if you feel like there is something burning inside of you, something that wants more for your family, your life, your income, and relationships, then you are exactly who this book is for.

Being raised in the church, I always focused on my faith in God. However, I felt like there were some missing pieces to my puzzle. Why was I always broke? Why did I lack fulfillment? Why did life always seem like such a struggle? And did I have to choose between faith and success, or could I have both?

Perhaps, like me, you wonder if things can truly be better, or different. Maybe you have questions about why the years are just slipping by, maybe you've fallen into a rut, or you're repeating what feels like the same years over and over again. Or maybe you have unanswered questions about people, leadership, God, your church, or money (or lack thereof) that plague your mind and leave you scratching your head.

Well, my friend, my COMMITMENT to you is I will talk about EVERYTHING 👄. I'm going to rip the Band Aid off of the untouchable topics 😦—the ones your parents may have thought were "taboo," the thought patterns unknowingly programmed into many of us about faith and money. I will go to a place of authenticity that most pastors, parents, or mentors won't. You will find brutally honest truths about my own downfalls. And I do this to give you an inside look at my life and journey, a window into how I went from a broke church boy, considering ending my own life and marriage, to adopting a millionaire mindset and setting my family up to win.

So, read at your own risk . . . Just know, I make no apologies for my success and how I have accomplished it. In fact, I lay it out for you step by step in *Church Boy To Millionaire*. This is my story, and these are the ACTION steps I took to speak fluent SUCCESS without compromising my faith.

CHAPTER ONE

LET'S FACE IT, LIFE CAN SUCK SOMETIMES

Winter of 2007 was the darkest season of my life.

You see, I faced $220,000 in unsecured debt. My mom had cancer and was in the hospital undergoing a stem cell transplant. The transmission had just gone out on my Nissan Armada with only 62,000 miles (and it wasn't covered under warranty). Two days later, someone broke into our house and stole thousands of dollars in possessions and our only running car.

On top of that, I was trying to keep so many secrets (mainly how bad it all really was) from my wife (trying to protect her and my kids but mostly trying to protect me). I was in complete denial that I was losing it all and had failed as a father and husband. I didn't know how I was going to make payroll for my thirteen employees at my furniture business. And I couldn't even afford rent for a store covered in "Going Out of Business!" signs.

My cell phone had been ringing off the hook from more creditors than you could ever imagine. In the months leading up to Christmas, I had even considered taking my own life. Physically, I was heavier than I had ever been. But to everyone around me, I was still the go-to guy, putting a fake smile on my face and just trying to make it through another day.

The very few people I did talk to didn't know how to help me, as they had never been in that deep before. Or they would say, "You will figure it out. Keep your head up." Like I had it all together. Yeah, right. They didn't have a clue how bad it really was. I was hiding so much. People said

things like, "Doug, I'm praying for you," and "It's just a season, bro." But honestly I didn't blame them. They didn't know how to help me—and frankly I didn't know how to help myself.

I felt guilt and shame, and truly hated myself for putting my family in a situation like this, where it looked like I was going to fail us all. I limped into church on Sundays, painting fake smile after fake smile on my face. You know, like the ones we all see all over social media, where everyone has a perfect life, perfect marriage, perfect job, and perfect date nights? The truth was, I was falling apart inside. The message at church was another one about keeping the faith, or the best is yet to come, blah blah blah . . . But inside I was saying *if you only knew*, 'cuz deep down I was a lonely man tired of living a facade. Spiritually, I was even questioning God and his existence.

I didn't even know my kids, as I practically missed Baby Kate's birth due to company demands. I was missing more dance recitals than I was proud to admit. I couldn't go because I worked so much—you might as well have called my wife a single mom. Let's face it, I was missing out on LIFE! Just to see my kids, my wife had to deliver fast food to my furniture store for my dinner because I was still working late into the night and past the girls' bedtime. Why? Because I couldn't afford to hire anyone. But the work needed to be done.

You see, I was stuck in what had become my own American Dream but it now felt more like an American Nightmare. I was truly trapped on a hamster wheel and couldn't get off. I knew that neither this season, nor my life, could go on like this much longer. The man inside was dying and the scary part was my hope was dying with him. Change had better come soon. And little did I know it was going to, just not the way I thought.

HOW DID I GET HERE?

It was a typical day, that December 27, while everyone was getting ready for work, I was the first one into my retail furniture store. Another year to pray for a #NewYearNewYou. Time for another faith harvest. Time for another fast. And the list of all the church and faith things many of us do could go on. And I'm sure you know what I'm talking about—I literally wanted to throw up. I was just sick of repeating the same year over and over, and the same pathetic prayers.

So, this was another morning of pacing and praying in the back of my furniture store at 5 a.m., like I did every day. Praying for a miracle or bailout, or sometimes crying for one. But on this particular day, something was different. It was another rainy, cloudy, Oregon morning. But in my prayer, I was half angry, half crying. And actually, very confused. I kept asking, "Why God? Why God . . . Why God?" Mostly the sadness that comes from years and years of begging for a miracle that seems to never come.

I'll never forget that red carpet in the back of my furniture store. In my anger and tears, I felt uncontrollably weak so I literally fell to my knees as the song "Hungry" by Kutless played over the sound system. I had been praying for four years for something to break through. I had prayed for a blessing and a financial miracle. But doors kept closing.

I had said no to many opportunities. Myself, my pride, and my ego were too tied to making my dream work and making my family and business successful. I was determined that I was going to build this thing, and God was going to bless it. As my knees buckled, I fell on my face in desperation and literally pounded the red carpet with my fist. And for the first time all I could say were the words, "I quit . . . I quit . . . I quit."

I sobbed uncontrollably on the floor. Here's a grown man, 265 pounds, yelling out, "I quit, God. I quit!" I honestly didn't know what I was quitting on, I just knew I was done. I would rather go work for a fast-food joint and have my family back than stay in the mess I was in with multiple zeros.

As I was bawling my eyes out and saying "I quit," I heard God say, "I know . . . I've just been waiting for you to say it. Because I was done with this season three years ago."

WHAT YOU DON'T KNOW

See, what you don't know is that two weeks before, all I wanted was a bailout. I looked for every possible way to cut corners. Looking back, this was a perpetual habit loop of mine. I was so used to cutting corners that when the corners didn't work, I was always looking for my "get out of jail free" card. It appeared that many people around me were finding blessing and growth, and honestly, I was sick of it.

I was living in such desperation. But what I didn't know is that there was a different path for me. And had I gotten the bailout I wanted, I would not be writing this book today. I'd be on a completely wrong path. Because this would've paved the way for five or ten more years of building the "empire of Doug," the numbers, my ego, and putting my family through more hell. Because I was trying to make something work that was never going to.

You see, through that season of desperation, I picked my favorite athlete of all time (and still to this day), the pro golfer Phil Mickelson, and watched what kind of money he made on Sundays. I knew that just 20 percent of the earnings he made on just one of his Sunday wins would solve all of my problems—and it would have. So, I wrote him a sad, pathetic, puppy-dog letter asking for a handout.

Don't believe me? Oh yes, my friends, it's sad but so true.

THANKS, PHIL

So, Phil Mickelson, I want to personally thank you for one of three possibilities:

1. Maybe my letter never reached you. Maybe an assistant or agent got it but never gave it to you.
2. Or maybe you did get this letter, but you never read it.
3. Or maybe the letter made it to you, and you did read it. But you didn't cut a check to some kid in desperation when you could have. If you had, it would've ruined me.

Whatever the case, thank you.

What I didn't know then, but now do, was that the money Phil was making on Sundays was actually earned on Mondays, Tuesdays, and Wednesdays when no one saw him working, practicing, and grinding for tournaments. Phil is known to have the best short game of all time. His practice intensity is legendary, and he spends the most time working on his game when no one is watching. That's why he can show up, compete, and still win to this day.

We see all these athletes and artists win, but we only see their highlight reels. We don't see the blood, sweat, and tears behind the stage. They're working their butts off to get that jacket, trophy, Grammy, and everything else. And that's the biggest lesson I received. Because in that season of quitting my agenda and getting back on God's, I learned He was actually looking to restore my family instead of give me a bailout.

SILOED LIVES

You see, my wife, Thea, and I lived siloed lives the first ten years of our marriage. We had our church friends, work friends, high-school friends, and our family. We shared a bank account. She did her role of cooking, cleaning, and raising the kids. I did mine of trying to fill up the bank account, pay the bills, and provide a life for us. But rarely would we have a family dinner at the table beyond Sundays. Or we would go out to dinner where both of us would spend more time staring at our phones than talking to each other. We would show up to church on Sundays looking happy, the girls in their nice jeans or dresses. We'd greet everyone. And then we'd start the whole process over again the next week.

I didn't realize that God was trying to lead me to an INTEGRATED LIFE. Now, what is an integrated life? It means all parts becoming one.

Imagine a life in which you and your spouse wake up together and are DREAMING again. You're talking about what great things could be next, rather than how you're going to pay the bills. You're taking the kids to school. There are weekends in which there's nothing to do but laugh and truly raise your family.

What would that feel like?

Well, after I said "I quit," my financial picture didn't get better for a while, but my relationships did. That process allowed me to get repurposed for what mattered most. It made it possible for me to go, be, and do what our family wanted to, and not just where a job or income told us to. What happened next was our family became FREE—free to be the family who was integrated, free to stop keeping score of who did what, and from hiding things from each other.

We got on the same page as a couple, and then as a family. We reestablished some non-negotiables, renewed some family values, and committed to figuring out the process and creating our best life. Whatever that was, it was going to be done as a family, and we would be in harmony. We didn't know how we were going to make it, but we were either going down together, or making it together.

So, my friend, I'm not sure where you are in your personal life, finances, needs, or what else might be going on. However, if you are asking, wishing, hoping, praying, and waiting for your bailout—*or for someone to come save you*—I'm here to tell you, no one's coming to bail you out. This one is going to be on you. It will require some CONTENDING, GRIT, HUSTLE, PRAYER, INNOVATIVE ideas, and 100 percent COMMITMENT.

I can fully admit now, a bailout would've ruined me and my family and the process I needed to go through. We can't shortcut growth. Phil Mickelson couldn't have written a check that would have changed my life. It would've been another temporary fix to my temporary commitment of just staying over broke. It would have kept me in unhealthy patterns and continued me on a path that would have ultimately ruined me.

I'm not sure what your current situation looks like, but I don't believe you are here by accident. Nor, just like I promised in my warning, if I had wanted to just be your friend and help you feel good, would I have opened up with such a heavy subject. However, the only reason I'm writing this book today is because I never got a bailout, and I had to bail myself out. In order for things to change, I had to accept my personal responsibilities to start the process of breakthrough for me and my family.

And I know for a fact you are not reading this by mistake, and if you are praying, wishing, or in a similar situation at all to where I was, then I'm letting you know there can be and will be freedom ahead. However, we are both fully aware that life can suck sometimes, but it's the process that makes us. Let's navigate this process together.

WHEN PRAYER AND ACTION COLLIDE

What are you praying for that you have not taken action on or said YES to? Did you know it could be right in front of you? ACT, my friends, ACT! It's not complicated. Staying in our heads or thinking that things have to be— *or will ever be*—perfect for good things to happen is a complete lie. If you're doing it right, it's going to seem messy! But it will be worth it! Clarity, results, growth, and breakthrough are waiting on the other side of ACTION!

"IN ORDER FOR
THINGS TO
IMPROVE,
WE MUST TAKE
PERSONAL
RESPONSIBILITY
AND ACCEPT
OUR CURRENT
REALITY."

—@THEREALDOUGWOOD
#CHURCHBOYTOMILLIONAIRE

CHAPTER TWO

CURRENT REALITY IS AN ACQUIRED TASTE

I'm unsure where you're at reading this book, and we still have a lot to talk about. But I'm here to tell you that I've been in many tough situations. I go through difficult things often and I'm still figuring it out with you. I am not writing this book as the expert. I'm writing to share with you that we are on this journey together. But I will tell you what has worked and give you some of the key steps I've taken to grow and stay on a healthy path.

What I had to do is take PERSONAL RESPONSIBILITY for my life, my family's life, my financial situation, my spiritual situation, and the integrity issues that slipped into my life. I knew they were unhealthy and keeping me stuck, so it was time to deal with them. Each of them has played a role. It's like a recipe, each ingredient affects the taste of the cake.

It was time to accept the hand I was dealt, the people who had screwed me, the people I'd been blaming, the ones talking behind my back, the ones who told me I wasn't good enough, and even those who thought I was the perfect Christian church boy 🙏.

I was here, and no one was going to get me out of it. It was time to accept the blessings in my life, the challenges in my situation. It was going to be up to me if my life was going to move forward.

Where are you right now in taking personal responsibility of your current situation? If you were to take an honest inventory of where you're at, what's going well, AND the challenges in your life, can you answer them honestly? And before you answer that, I want to let you know that current reality is an acquired taste.

I spent many years refusing to open the mail that held the credit card statements and bills I couldn't pay. It was easier to ignore them and screen the creditors' phone calls. I spent many years not stepping on a scale because I didn't want to see what I knew was probably true. I avoided the doctor like the plague, because honestly the embarrassment would've been too humbling. Even in good seasons of my marriage, the truth was that Thea and I swept everything we didn't want to deal with under the rug. We avoided the TRUTH until it was too late or all hell broke loose. And about four times a year, we would start threatening and saying words both of us wish we could take back.

LET'S TALK ABOUT YOU!

In order for things to move forward and improve, we must take a clear look at the current reality. Let's take our finances as an example. If our satisfaction level today with our overall finances is not where we want it, who's keeping it from moving to total satisfaction?

- *Is it my job?*
- *Is it my spouse's responsibility?*
- *Is it my boss's fault?*
- *Is my credit card interest rate too high?*
- *Is it my company's cutbacks?*
- *Is it because the company didn't give out bonuses this year?*

. . . and honestly, the list could go on. But really, who's keeping my finances from moving closer to overall satisfaction?

You are. No, seriously, you are. No one is going to change it but you.

Now I want you to apply this same lesson to other important areas in your life where you're unsatisfied. Ask, "Who is responsible?"

I'll save you the trouble: you are.

Yes, all of the above can play a factor. But the truth is, we must take personal responsibility and accept our current reality. No, we might not like it. Yes, it's ugly. But are we ready to do something about it, break through, and change ourselves? Change our families, our kids, and the people we care about? And honestly, the people who need us the most, including our families, need us at our best!

DOUGISM #2

TAKE PERSONAL RESPONSIBILITY

When you choose to take personal responsibility, you become free. When I did this in my own life, I also had to leave a few "I'm sorry" messages with unreturned phone calls. I'm OK with that. I knew I needed to own my part, take personal responsibility for my actions, and expect nothing in return. Always VALUE your own FREEDOM and PEOPLE over anything else. I didn't say you need to be close friends again. However, releasing hard feelings, breaking down walls that got built, and letting go of assumptions that got made are important for healing and freedom to begin. Give it a try and watch what happens.

Deep down inside, I know we all want to better mankind and leave our communities, churches, friends, and families in better places.

So, I'll say it one more time, my friends, current reality is an acquired taste. And the reason we're talking about this first is that it's important we get brutally honest with our current situation. We have grown up in a world in which plenty of people say, "Your situation is okay. It's normal. It'll work itself out. The best is yet to come. Just take a day off. Look at the positives." . . . and the list could go on. This type of advice has some great positive thinking, but it's very rarely true.

WHEN GOOD THINGS COME

My friends, I will be blunt and tell you what most of your friends or family either don't know, or won't tell you, simply because we're living in a world filled with hype, false hope, fantasy, and a "let's just keep prayin' about it" mentality. But the truth is, nothing's changed, has it? I now like to pray like it depends on God, but I WORK like it depends on me.

Someone has probably told you multiple times, like they told me, "Good things come to those who wait." Frankly, I think we're at a place where we can call bull 💩. How's it been working out? I can tell you it hasn't worked well for me. Instead, I've learned this: *good things come to those who take action!*

I reached a point a few years ago where I was where you might be at right now. Someone told me this, and I'm gonna tell you right now, it was incredible advice: "Not one person but myself will make, break, or define my success besides me—only me!" (Now, please resist over-spiritualizing this—I know God plays a key role in all of this for many of us. But we have to take action for breakthrough to happen!)

So, are we at the point where we can honestly say, "It's not my uncle, my wife, my business partner, my pastor, or whomever else we want to insert into this statement (you know who I'm talking about) that is responsible for my family's success but me."

If it's going to be, it's entirely up to me.

With this comes my next question for you: What would life look like with an ABUNDANCE in each of those areas? (More on abundance in Chapter 6.) And I seriously mean this.

- *What is a marriage and family 10 to you?*
- *What is a financial 10 to you?*
- *What is a physical health 10 to you?*
- *What is a spiritual 10 to you?*
- *What is a purpose 10 to you?*

Before you start backtracking on me and head into what you DON'T believe and you DON'T think, I want you to tune out anything anyone has ever said to you. Because the mess I was in just eight years ago wouldn't have allowed myself to think that the life, marriage, finances, fulfillment, and family I have now are even possible.

I personally understand how hard it is to DREAM again when you feel like you're so deep in the mud. And maybe you're not in the mud, and you're not where I was in 2007, but wherever you are, I believe you want to get better and create an amazing life for those who matter most to you.

So, I'm going to ask you some big questions only you can answer in the following areas:

In the next twelve months, WHAT do you want?
What do you really want? Please be specific.

In the next twelve months, WHY do you want it?
This is about you. I don't care how selfish it sounds. Be totally honest, without any self-judgment. This is YOUR why, and nobody else's.

WHO will benefit when you've accomplished it?
It might be your family, kids, coming generations, community, church, or any-one else you care about.

I acknowledge how hard that may have been for some of you. The first time I answered these questions, it took me over an hour to get transparent with myself. I didn't realize I had turned off the ability to dream or think things could ever be different for me or my family, Also, if you're trying to figure some of them out still, it's okay. It's a process. You are completely normal, and this takes time. Seriously, congratulations on getting honest with yourself. Now the real work begins.

All our lives, people have encouraged us to dream, pray, and believe that everything will get better. And they're right, things are going to get better—if we're ready to do what comes next.

Now, before I ask you the last question, remember: We now know what we want. We now know why we want it. And we now see whose lives will improve if we're successful. So now we ask the most difficult question of all, "What are WE willing to do to get it?"

Here's what it looked like for me.

WHAT ARE WE WILLING TO DO?

Thea and I said we wanted a THRIVING marriage for many years. But I personally was unwilling to go to counseling and get some coaching. The truth was, we didn't have that bad of a marriage, but my pride, bullheaded-ness, and skepticism about counselors and coaches stood between Thea and I getting the support we needed. You see, I use to think you only go to a counselor when things got really bad. I actually discovered that with a "maintenance check," they could help us continue on the right path by making a few adjustments.

I used to wish for more money. And the truth was, I needed more money. But frankly, I wasn't willing to get creative, take a secondary job, start a side business, explore direct sales, or utilize current technology to get my family out of the financial situation we were in. Why not? Because my ego was holding me up.

I'll close with this, if you want to bring your marriage, your family, your finances, your spiritual life, your physical health, or anything else closer to a 10, answer this straight up: *Am I willing to do the WORK and take the ACTION to make it happen?*

Because, my friends, anything we want really badly is going to take WORK. I'm seeing way too many people taking the easy way out and thinking that the grass would be greener if they divorced or cashed it in. I'm not here to get into your business, but you did buy my book. And I'm just going to leave this right here: "Stop fantasizing about what it might be like if you left your spouse."

Buck up and do the freaking work on yourself and your marriage. CONTEND for your marriage. It's worth it. I almost walked out on Thea and the girls years ago and it would have been 100 percent selfish. That's what I had to confront. Now, what are you willing to do to move forward?

- *Are you willing to acknowledge your current reality?*
- *Are you willing to have the hard talk with your spouse?*
- *Are you willing to open up the bill drawer?*
- *Are you willing to call a family meeting?*
- *Are you willing to ask for support from someone you respect in an area you struggle?*
- *Are you tired of trying to lose the same 65 pounds every year?*
- *Are you willing to say no to what you want now and yes to what you really want long-term?*

My friends, this can all be accomplished, because I'm living proof that when you're ready to get real, you're tired of BS-ing yourself and the people around you, and you're ready to create more RESULTS than excuses,

BREAKTHROUGH can happen. But this thing is going to TAKE WORK. It's not going to happen overnight. Honestly, we're going to need to spend a few months together in this book working through it. And the upcoming chapters will lead you there.

Now, what ACTIONS are YOU willing to take to accomplish this?

When I decided to take personal responsibility, realized a bailout wasn't coming, and said "I quit" in 2007, I truly began the life I have today. From a monetary standpoint, my life didn't get any better for two more years. But during those two years, I discovered my purpose, my marriage and family relationships began to THRIVE, and I began to find clarity on what the future might look like.

My challenge to you, should you choose to accept it, is to acknowledge that this is going to take work, time, and probably even unlearning some habits that have been disserving you. It may take you seven weeks, seven months, or even seven years like it did for me. But if you commit to the process of being honest with your CURRENT REALITY, keeping your goals clearly in front of you, and getting absolutely obsessive with the action steps to accomplish them, you will begin to experience freedom like you have never experienced before.

BONUS RESOURCE

In order to move FORWARD and IMPROVE, take a clear look at your CURRENT REALITY in four key areas. Get your free bonus resource, the **Current Reality Assessment**, by visiting ChurchBoyToMillionaire.com

WIN THE DAY

———

Often, when I lay my head on my pillow at night, I ask myself, "Who WON the day, me and my ACTIONS or my excuses and procrastination?" Be honest with yourself and evaluate. Current reality is an acquired taste. Sip on it and you will like it, as long as you're willing to do something about it and take action.

Win the day! Even if you're only winning four out of every seven days, I guarantee YOU are gaining ground and will achieve massive success and growth. It's the slight edge and the small things that separate breaking down or breaking through!

I encourage you to not beat yourself up. We are in full control of our ACTIONS! Own your zone! If today beat you, own, dominate, and win tomorrow!

"LIFE HAPPENS.
WE MUST TAKE
PERSONAL
RESPONSIBILITY
FOR WHAT WE
CAN CONTROL,
AND NOT REACT
TO THINGS
WE CAN'T."

—@THEREALDOUGWOOD
#CHURCHBOYTOMILLIONAIRE

CHAPTER THREE

BOSS UP

Are you a VICTIM of ATTACK thinking? Have you ever met someone who always seems to be the victim in every situation? In the church world, it's often coded as I'm "under attack" from the enemy. Well, if you would have met me eight years ago, I was the victim of my own choices.

Maybe you know someone like this, or perhaps this is you. It's often used as a term in faith communities that serves the below-the-line thinking club (I will explain what this is shortly) and it's usually keeping people from massive breakthrough!

Here are a couple things to think about if you are a reoccurring victim of daily, weekly, or monthly spiritual ATTACK.

First, maybe it's become a badge of honor, or worse yet an EXCUSE, of why things that you are in 100 percent control of like your health, finances, and life aren't improving. It's obviously someone else's fault! But, before I go any farther, I'm aware that LIFE happens to all of us. Some things are beyond our control. However, how we choose to respond in every situation is 100 percent within our control.

For instance, as I write this book right now, I could easily say my computer is "under attack." It's currently 1:28 a.m. I'm at the Breakthrough Loft in North Scottsdale overlooking the city, and my laptop keeps giving me the spinning wheel of death. My document keeps reloading itself and it takes forever to find my place every 45 minutes. The truth is, I probably just need to update my computer. I probably need to close applications at night and treat it with a little better care. It probably needs a good restart.

Seriously, some of us would say, "Oh my goodness, Doug, this is a spiritual attack!" Maybe this book is NOT supposed to be written, or others would say, "Wow, Doug, this is going to be amazing because your computer is 'under attack.'" No, my friends, life happens and computers crash. It's just called reality. I don't overfeed negativity and put energy here.

Now, I'm not poking fun at anyone who does this, I just want to offer a different perspective. But are you getting my point?

Sometimes technology fails. Sometimes computers need to reboot. Sometimes my aminos spill on the computer keyboard (as they did just an hour ago)! But my friends, I'm not under attack. Frankly, I would encourage you to stop giving Satan so much credit.

WHICH SIDE OF THE CROSS ARE WE ON?

For my faith-following friends, which side of the cross are we on? The battle was won and the price was paid at the cross, right?! So how can we be under attack all the time?! God sent his son and he took care of the battles, saying, "It is finished!"

Take off your grave clothes and walk in life and the victory of the resurrection. This is choosing to live a faith walk that's above the line.

Now, I'm not saying that spiritual attacks never happen—because I'm not that naive. But the point is, challenging times happen to us all. Car accidents, crashing computers, spilt aminos giving your computer a bath. . . Actually, I find that these scenarios offer a great opportunity to test our emotional intelligence to see how we handle life when we're thrown a curveball.

Stop overthinking and stop giving the Devil so much credit! Boss up your mindset. Winners win, and losers lose. Step into the winners circle. Winners are the ones who take personal responsibility, who admit that sometimes, life just happens. They don't complain on social media all the time about every little life scenario that happens. They stop in the moment, acknowledge what happened, and challenge any victimhood mindset, thoughts, or emotions. They simply move on without creating a drama post or a you-will-never-believe-what-just-happened post on their social media pages! It baffles me, because some people need drama like I need oxygen.

IT'S NOT YOUR FAULT (UNTIL IT IS)

Understand that if this is you, it's not your fault. You've most likely been conditioned by the below-the-line club (blamers, shamers, and people who always make excuses). Or maybe others grew up with (or still buy in to) victimhood teaching and preaching. The truth is, these same people often need attention. Or they wear the "attacks" as a badge of honor anytime LIFE gets hard.

However, here's where it does become your fault: if you continue to blame, shame, or play the victim card after understanding this. If this is so, I don't feel sorry for you 🤷. Remember, when we choose to change the way we look at things, the things we look at change.

LIFE happens to all of us. So it's 100 percent up to us to take PER-SONAL RESPONSIBILITY for what we can control and not react emotionally to the things we can't control. How we deal with anything and everything that happens to us—or for us—is up to us. It's up to us to CHOOSE to change our habits, circumstances, relationships, or move beyond the recurring hardships in our lives.

For the followers of Christ out there, like myself, let's remember that our power and dominion over every situation was handled at the cross 2,000 years ago. It should also be left at the cross. If Satan is truly under our feet, let's act like it and stop giving him so much credit. If the spirit of the LIVING GOD is in and among us, then the battle is already WON.

People are giving the Devil way too much credit and power over their lives. Worse, when they believe he got them into the mess they're in, they'll stay stuck there! God loves you, but Satan doesn't care that much about you and has already moved on—and so should you.

DON'T ROLL YOUR EYES!

Let's stop the madness and take back our power. For my American friends, we live in a first-world country but sometimes we act like we should be on the receiving end of everyone else's charity! Or that we deserve constant condolences for our bad choices. Let's boss up, level up, and own our zones 🙌 !!!

People often talk about how others affect them. "So and so" pushes my buttons. OK, fine, maybe "So and so" makes you mad, sad, or scared. But why does that person have so much power over you? Or WHY do you have buttons to push? Who's life is it? Yours or theirs? Take your POWER BACK!

If your health is constantly "under attack," there are some likely habits in your life that make these issues symptoms of poor behaviors. You are not under attack—you're experiencing the consequences of bad behavior. Let's change the behavior and see what improves. And, let's be honest, sometimes accidents happen and it's called LIFE. But we can learn through every adversity, setback, and relationship and truly GROW.

If your finances are always "under attack," stop spending money on stuff you don't need. Find a way to increase your income. There are plenty of companies hiring for side jobs. Start a stay-at-home business. Drive Uber or Lyft. Get a side hustle. And no, you're not above it!

(By the way, most people I know with a side hustle enjoy it more than their day job and make an even bigger impact while they're at it.)

Here's the truth, if you are this far into this book but are rolling your eyes, thinking only a few people get lucky, well brother (or sister), I used to do the same thing, until I set my ego aside and opened my mind to alternative ways of making INCOME . . . until I listened to my wife, because she was actually onto many good things 😜.

You see, up until a few years ago, I was waiting for my big break. In complete transparency, my breakthrough only came AFTER I took total personal responsibility and confronted my beasts. I stopped blaming everyone else, then worked on myself, my emotions, and my spirit. Honestly, I worked my @$$ off to create a better life for my family and myself!

I'll say again, if it's going to be, it will be up to me and I am the ONLY PERSON who can change my current situation.

#SORRYNOTSORRY

Recently, I saw someone wearing a shirt that read, "Nobody cares, work harder!" Lots of TRUTH to that! However, I think people really do care (at least I do). What they're tired of is hearing others talk about the same song, different verse, but seeing no changes in your actions.

It breaks my heart to see amazing people choosing to play small, or choosing to stay victims of life or Satan. My encouragement to you is take YOUR AUTHORITY back. Join me in playing and LIVING a life ABOVE THE LINE. Break with blame, shame, and woe-is-me thinking. Start TAKING PERSONAL RESPONSIBILITY.

When we choose to take back our power, we'll notice massive changes in many areas. In fact, even the way we pray will change. My friends, let's stop being victims and take back our power. Let's stop blaming, shaming, and making excuses and take 100 percent responsibility. Let's stop struggling and start contending. Let's stop trying and start choosing. Let's stop whining and start acting.

So here's my question for you, which side of the cross are you living on?

DOUGISM #4

RAISE YOUR COMMITMENT

If we are short on creativity it's because we lack commitment. When we lack commitment, we will lack passion, creativity, and desire! Raise your COMMITMENT level, and you will quickly find greater creativity in implementing ACTION to reach your goals. However, nothing starts without being absolutely OBSESSED and PASSIONATE with what you want most. You must be truly committed to it. Get clear on what you actually want, don't apologize for WHY you want it, and take the ACTIONS to get it.

CHAPTER FOUR

IT'S OKAY TO QUIT

It was May of 2007. Bills were piling up. Customers at my furniture store were getting angry. I had their money but I couldn't get them their furniture. Every text message was a problem or a complaint. I loved my kids but spent no time with them. I was just trying to keep my company alive. At this point, all I was doing was just trying to keep from losing my house, losing my faith, and frankly, losing my 💩.

My coping, my just-trying-to-keep-things-afloat behavior, was my secret addiction to pornography I thought nobody knew about. It was my secret hiding place. It gave me just enough dopamine per day to escape the pain of what was going on. It let me hide what felt like my business, my life, my marriage, my finances, and my faith slipping away—and I didn't know how to stop.

In fact, I almost left my wife (but am so glad I didn't). I personally found that pornography puts ideas and desires in your mind to chase tail you shouldn't be chasing, versus chasing your dreams, your wife, your kids, your purpose, and your finances. It puts you living in a fantasy versus doing the hard work, and the heart work, on yourself.

Let me take a moment here to be very clear, though. My use of pornography had nothing to do with a lack of fulfillment in my wife or her beauty. My wife, Thea, is absolutely one of the most beautiful woman in the world (and I'm not just saying that as her husband). Many of you reading this know her, and also know her spirit shines as bright as her beauty. This was a ME issue and I had fallen into a trap that I didn't know how to get out of.

Women, I also want to tell you that pornography has nothing to do with you. Your personal appearance does not drive us men to pornography—we unfortunately find it on our own.

Sadly, it's hyper-addicting and one of the easiest vices to hide, to access, and to feel like you're in control of. It starts off small, but gets worse. It leads to depression, loneliness, and guilt. I hated the person I became when porn had control of me. I accept full responsibility for my own challenges. It's something I have contended against in my life, my kids' lives, and in my marriage. I'm standing in freedom today, but I don't act like I have it all figured out either, because it's a beast I continue to confront (more on this in Chapter 5). I keep our home, phones, and computers protected with software to stay accountable because I know I'm still human.

REPURPOSING SEASON

You see, though, that season of my life got even worse than that. I had just visited a bankruptcy attorney and learned that not all of my debt was bankruptable. So, I dug up my $1,000,000 life insurance policy to find out if it had a suicide clause. I was relieved to see that after the first year, there was not. I realized I was worth more dead than alive. You're telling me I could take my life, then my wife and girls would be set up with $750,000? I entertained this more seriously than I care to admit.

My friends, the next two years were a blur. All I know is I didn't quit. I kept praying, hustling, putting payroll on my personal credit card and working all the hours it took to just make it another week. I'm here to tell you, if for some reason you're in a dark place or anywhere near where I was, don't quit on your life, your marriage, your kids, or yourself.

You're in a season of repurposing which will lead to so much fulfillment, happiness, and joy. I know you can't see around the corner right now. I couldn't either. But I promise you, if you are still reading, you're on the right track if you apply what I'm saying.

If you read Chapter 1, you know what happened at the end of that year. I made it by saying, "I quit." I quit fighting for a business (or ministry) that was no longer meant to be. I became willing to lose it all. Why? So that I could step fully into my purpose. So that I could unleash breakthrough for my family and those around me.

FULFILLMENT FACTOR

My friend, where is your fulfillment factor? Are you ready to find it? Discover it? Or get back to it? Now, I'm not going to paint a pretty facade on this next part. It may take doing something drastic, losing any amount of ego you have left, maybe even swallowing a spoonful of pride to stop carrying the front.

It's time to be repurposed.

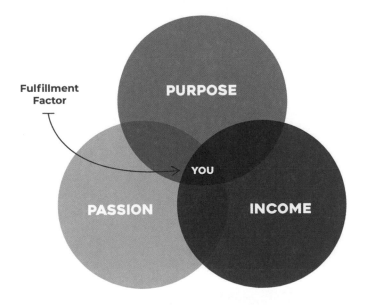

You and I both know that God has gigantic plans for you but we often lose sight of them or wonder if they are even real anymore. He says it in Jeremiah 29:11, but lately I know it seems like just another verse you might not even believe anymore. But if you're ready to do the HEART work, and not just the HARD work, this next season holds larger impact and massive restoration when you pursue where your purpose, passion, and income potential align.

I'm just going to ask you a few questions to help you move into more fulfillment. And if the shoe fits, wear it! Because nobody can make these decisions, or give you clarity on your purpose, besides you.

Is your current job fulfilling?	*1 2 3 4 5 6 7 8 9 10*
Has your ministry started feeling like a job?	*1 2 3 4 5 6 7 8 9 10*
Do you dread Monday mornings?	*1 2 3 4 5 6 7 8 9 10*
Are you a serial T.G.I.F.er?	*1 2 3 4 5 6 7 8 9 10*
Are you paid what you're worth?	*1 2 3 4 5 6 7 8 9 10*
Have you said no to a second stream of income?	*1 2 3 4 5 6 7 8 9 10*
Are you continually carrying financial weight, year after year?	*1 2 3 4 5 6 7 8 9 10*
Have you outgrown your welcome?	*1 2 3 4 5 6 7 8 9 10*
Is your time up?	*1 2 3 4 5 6 7 8 9 10*
Are you ready to pass the torch?	*1 2 3 4 5 6 7 8 9 10*
Are you holding onto something that is someone else's dream for you?	*1 2 3 4 5 6 7 8 9 10*
Is there family pressure to stay?	*1 2 3 4 5 6 7 8 9 10*
Have you been guilted into staying?	*1 2 3 4 5 6 7 8 9 10*
Are you sick of chasing after the carrot?	*1 2 3 4 5 6 7 8 9 10*
Are you tired of running on a hamster wheel?	*1 2 3 4 5 6 7 8 9 10*
Is somebody controlling your time and money?	*1 2 3 4 5 6 7 8 9 10*
Are you building your dream or someone else's?	*1 2 3 4 5 6 7 8 9 10*

If your honest answer to any of the above surprised you, caused you to rethink, or even question where you're at today, it's okay. Please understand that you are normal. But you, and only YOU, have the ability to make the change you want to see in your life. Now, here's the path.

YOUR PATH

Answer the following questions, and answer them as honestly as possible:

- *What are you doing when you are most fulfilled?*
- *What brings you the most joy?*
- *What do you like doing?*
- *What do you feel like you are good at?*

My friend, we live in a day and age where technology is advancing at an accelerated rate. You have the ability to take whatever you want to do, whatever idea you have, or whatever need you've found that is unmet, and turn it into MASSIVE INCOME, PURPOSE, and FULFILLMENT. How? Social media is free! You can take your UNIQUE ABILITY, that thing that brings you fulfillment, and start sharing it in a way that will change your life.

It's time to start impacting lives, making more money, and doing what you're best at every single day. Now, I'm fully aware this process will take time. It will take seeking wise counsel, prayer, conversations with your spouse, careful thought, and exploring all options. But frankly, while it will take some time, the decisions need to be made now.

I can tell you in 2007 when I quit, I had going-out-of-business signs on my door within four weeks. I had everything lined up, planned, and executed on. I was preparing for six months of more hell, but I knew I had to start the process. The DECISION had to be made, then acted upon.

So, I encourage you, my friend, make the decision to chase fulfillment. Even if you're unclear on what's next, even if you're still questioning your purpose. The one thing you do have clarity on is that things can't continue the way they are. And that's okay. I've found that God has spoken to me and given me more strength in the in-between—the place some call the desert.

Here's what I discovered: I wanted my PASSION back. My wife needed her husband back. My kids needed their dad back. But please know I'm not talking about my living shell—my spirit had died. I'd lost who I once was, and I decided to give anything to get it back.

And you know what? My wife got back a husband who was stronger than ever. But I'll tell you, I'm thankful she didn't give up. She kept PRAY-ING and BELIEVING and giving me the nudge—and I don't know if you have anyone giving you a nudge, but you can do this babe 😜. (And I'm sorry dudes if I just called you a babe.)

My kids have a full-time father again. I'll never forget when they said, "Papa, you're so happy." Baby Katelyn can't remember when I worked out-

side of the home. All she knows is a Dad who's at home as much as her mother.

It's okay to quit sometimes, as long as you're quitting on the right things and a season is fin-ished, as long as you quit build-ing the wrong empire, or bring an end to a season you know needs to be finished. Obviously, I'm not a psychic, I can't tell you what's next. But if you've made it this far, you're on the right track.

You can do this. Hold strong and make the DECISION. I said "I QUIT" and it was the best thing ever!

DOUGISM #5

FREE YOURSELF

———

When you understand that NO ONE IS coming to save you or your family—AND THIS LIFE IS 100 PERCENT YOUR RESPONSIBILITY—YOU SET YOURSELF FREE!

CHAPTER FIVE

CONFRONT THE BEAST

Before we dive in, I have to apologize to my Mom. In 1978, she had to push a 10.5 pound baby named Douglas between her legs. Sorry, Mom 😵.

Let's face it, I was always a big kid. I spent my life being called "big-boned." But that's not the worst one. The worst was being called "husky." Now, I could get over the husky comments. But what I could not get over is why in the hell my mom bought me jeans labeled husky?! Dude, you're killing me 😫! It was even printed on the belt loop tag so EVERYONE could see. Not a fun fashion moment for me.

I kid you not, I had to wear huskies until the eighth grade. These things were brutal. (Thankfully, I just completed a twelve-step program for husky survivors—and I think I'm going to be okay.) Parents, if your kid is big-boned like I was, please never make them wear pants labeled "husky." They will need counseling, so help a kid out and find something else.

While I'm going down memory lane, does anyone remember half-shirts from the '80s? I sure do.

HUSKY IN A HALF-SHIRT

In second grade, my family went to a church picnic at Rogers Park in Forest Grove, Oregon. Keep in mind, for those of you watching at home, I was still in the middle of the Husky Movement. Now, we pulled up to the picnic like any other bright, sunny Sunday afternoon. And the moment I jump from the car, my Mom hands me a bag with my play clothes. Then she gave me marching orders to change into them in the park bathroom.

Now, while I'm giving advice, parents, please don't send your kids into park bathrooms alone—even for a ten year old, a lot of dark things have happened there 😱. But I digress . . . I walk into the bathroom trying to tiptoe through the pools of water that always seem to be in them, then pull out my play clothes so I can get out into the action.

To my horror, my Mom had issued me a pair of nylon, nut-hugger shorts and a half-shirt. Mom, seriously, why? Half-shirts were made for grown men with abs, like Apollo Creed from *Rocky* 👊. But this ten year-old had zero—and I mean ZERO—business wearing one. The picture proves my point.

So there I was, dressing in this park bathroom where it looked like something very violent had taken place in the toilet earlier, and I'm doing everything I can to stretch my half-shirt into a full-shirt to get somewhat close to my nut-huggers—but it wasn't working.

The story gets worse. So, I waddle out half-holding on to my stretched-out shirt, going out to play with all the other kids. During a game of tag, I tripped and fell on a gravel path. Oh yes. Now here is the fat kid in the half shirt bleeding with HUGE strawberry railroad tracks all over my exposed belly. Oh yes, this is a memory I will never forget ☺.

Truthfully, I had a mother who loved me so much, she never viewed me as fat. Mom, you know how much I love you, and I know how much you love me. I think we can all agree, a mother's love looks at who you are and sees the best in you—but sometimes doesn't see what's really going on. To this day, she and I chuckle about these moments. And she says, "Doug, I never knew you were a big kid, you were just my son."

HOW YOU REALLY SEE YOURSELF

There's a great lesson here. Maybe you have people around you saying, "You're an amazing pastor" or "Oh my gosh, you're such an incredible dad!" "You're the sweetest lady I've ever met." "You're such a gifted communicator!" "You're so talented." "You're an amazing coach," or "I could never do what you do!" And the list goes on. But how many of us actually believe those compliments? The truth is, many of us don't think we're any of the things other people see.

I heard those things for years, but all along I wanted to scream out, "If you only knew how I *really* feel!" Inside, there was a boy crying out that didn't want to be fat anymore.

As the years go by, we all get better at burying the things of our past. For some of us, it was a childhood weight issue 🖼. For others of us, it was a hurtful comment we'll never forget. And for others, it was something else that we really don't want to talk about—with anyone.

CONFRONTING OUR BEASTS

If I asked you right now, what area or pattern of your life keeps repeating itself, what would you say? Your weight? Your integrity? Your confidence? Your intelligence? Isolation? Self-comparison? Jealousy? Pride? Your financial habits? Your relationship habits? Drama? Negativity? Or anything else?

You see, we're really good at ignoring these repeating insecurities and issues. Often, we even convince ourselves they don't affect our jobs, ministries, income, spiritual lives, marriages, or family relationships. But the truth is, this repeating issue is probably what's holding you up the most.

Another way of looking at it is, what are you constantly ignoring, avoiding, or always asking for advice, support, and prayer for? Now, before you throw this book across the room, please hear my heart on this. I call these repeating issues *beasts*.

My friends, it's time we CONFRONT OUR BEASTS. The beasts we're IGNORING and AVOIDING. I chose to face a few of mine by looking at them straight in the mirror. They are ugly to admit and to face head on. Change can't happen until we confront the beast that is breaking us.

I'll be brutally honest with you. As an adult, in my darkest seasons, my health was increasingly out of control. I could try, hope, and pray, but I wasn't doing anything about it. At my heaviest, 265 pounds, I drug myself home from a hard day at 8 p.m., would barely take a moment to kiss my daughters, Amaya and Kate, and then be passed out in front of the TV by 9 p.m. with a food hangover. The truth was, the beast I kept ignoring was my weight. And it was wreaking havoc on me, my company, my wife, my girls, my finances, and even my spiritual health.

This is what beasts do. They are issues that work their way through generations. For all of us, in order for breakthrough to take place, we've got to get brutally honest with ourselves. This means naming and confronting what we know is there.

As a coach, here are some of the most common beasts that seem to hold people up the most. The great part is that for many who have confronted these things head on, they now have extreme FREEDOM and are THRIVING today because they were willing to do something about it.

- *Debt*
- *Anger*
- *Secret addiction*
- *Physical health and weight*
- *Fear of people's opinions*
- *Excuses*
- *Excessive need for approval*
- *Abuse of alcohol or drugs*
- *Prescription pills*
- *Secrets from spouse or family*
- *Pride*
- *Need to be right all the time*
- *Ego*
- *Need for control*
- *Inability to apologize*
- *Inability to accept personal responsibility*
- *Abusive language towards others*
- *Need for the spotlight*
- _____

DOUGISM #6

RECONCILIATION

I dare you to reconcile with someone whom you have sworn you never would. Pain points become PEACE points when we free ourselves up to heal and move on.

Now, I'm going to say this as nicely as I can: if you are serious about creating massive breakthrough in your life, organization, marriage, health, family, income, or whatever else you're looking to accomplish, the beast that stands out to you most on this page is what is holding you up. Like it, love it, hate it—I'm going to tell you the frickin' TRUTH.

"I NEED HELP"

In the summer of 2010, I confronted one of my fiercest beasts: my weight. So, I began a journey to lose 65 pounds. I knew this was an area I'd resisted and avoided for the longest time. For years, I'd tried—and failed. Tried—and failed. But do we really call dieting in secret and white-knuckling it for a week or two trying? I knew there had to be something better out there. So, I called a friend I knew was having success losing weight and keeping it off. I said the words that were the hardest to say, "I NEED HELP."

I'll spare you the details. But as brutal on my ego as it was, I knew nothing was going to change until I confronted the beast of my weight. I couldn't ignore it anymore. It stared me down in the mirror every morning. My wife deserved better. My kids deserved better. My God and the temple he gave me deserved better. And honestly, so did I. So, I chose to level up and become the best version of myself.

You see, while I lost 65 pounds physically, what I didn't expect was for the spirit within to come alive. A few weeks into the process, people were asking me what had changed and what had gotten into me. The truth was, I'd masked so much pain in food. It was a coping mechanism. I ate when I was sad, when I was happy. My friends and I celebrated and laughed with food. We'd mourn with food. We'd watch the game with food. I made all the jokes. Played the Tommy Boy role long enough. Beat everyone to the punchline. But finally, I made the change.

On this journey toward the best version of myself, I began to discover how unhealthy some of the people around me were—yes, even my family, my church friends and my pastor. During this process, I was laughed at, told I didn't need to lose weight, and that diets don't work. People in my friends, family, and church circle actually said things like: "You're just gonna gain it back," "Take it easy, chill out," "Doug, other people are feeling uncomfortable around you," "You need to chill out with this whole health thing."

That's when I realized how toxic some of my friends and family really were. I wasn't simply confronting my own beast—I was confronting a family beast, a culture beast, and frankly, a church beast.

BEASTS OF OUR BLOODLINES

You see, beasts have a funny sense of humor. Here's how they work: They convince us they don't need to be confronted. That you can live with them. That nobody needs to know about them. That you're the only one dealing with it, so no one can relate. And that nobody else is talking about their challenges, so you shouldn't either.

Here's the truth: *these are complete lies.*

In fact, if you get brutally honest with your bloodline, there is probably someone in your family that is (or has) been dealing with the exact thing you are. I know I'm getting personal with you here, but truthfully, it's just you and this book. No one knows what you're thinking about right now, I'm just holding up a broken mirror. We can look away and avoid it. Or we can CONFRONT it and take PERSONAL RESPONSIBILITY for it.

WHAT CAN WE DO?

So, we all have beasts, and you've now identified yours. I know you're scared, because you know it's time to confront them, too. It's time to do something about it, to reach out to someone you can trust, or even a professional who can help or guide you through this process. Don't go at it alone and resist the urge to isolate yourself. Resist the urge to stay silent.

1. **Step One:** Be willing to have conversations with the people your beast has affected—if it has at all.
2. **Step Two:** Accept personal responsibility and don't make excuses for it any longer. It's your issue, so prepare to take action immediately. Get some help, accountability, AND take action.
3. **Step Three:** Do it now—before you lose this emotion. You and the people who matter most are too important to wait. The longer you think about this and don't take action on it, the harder it will be to do. Some of you need to put the book down at this moment and get this process started.

When you've completed the process above, and start this journey of confronting your beast, I truly believe you'll unlock the path to your breakthrough—your spiritual, physical, and financial breakthrough—over YOU, your FAMILY, and your LEGACY.

CHANGING YOUR FAMILY TREE

There are things we love about our families. And also things we wish weren't there. I'm letting you know I'm here today writing this book because of the prayers of my parents and grandparents. Something that has helped Thea and I has been looking down both of our family bloodlines and asking those same questions. We decided together to create a new family tree.

To do this, we asked three questions. What blessings from our family heritage do we want to accept and continue passing down? What parts of our heritage do we need to acknowledge and reject, or maybe even confront (i.e. gossip, divorce, debt, addiction, etc.)?

Now I want you to look at your family tree. Take an inventory about what your parents, grandparents, and all of their relatives have ever been known for. Here are some questions to help you get started.

GENERATIONAL BLESSINGS

- *As far back as you can think, what has your family done well?*
- *Are you known for singing?*
- *Have you always owned businesses?*
- *What do you love about your family?*
- *What traditions have been passed down for generations?*
- *What financial wealth has your family achieved?*
- *What spiritual blessings does your family walk in?*
- *Has physical health been a constant in your family?*
- *What else is a positive quality passed down in your family?*

GENERATIONAL BEASTS

Now think back as far as you can about what your family challenges have been:

- *Is divorce a normal thing in your family?*
- *Is debt a common theme in your family?*
- *Is blame a common theme in your family?*
- *Is addiction to _____ a common theme?*
- *Is abuse a common theme in your family?*
- *Is the need for control a common theme in your family?*
- *Is the keeping of unhealthy secrets a common theme in your family?*
- *Is a pattern of hiding harmful behaviors a common theme in your family?*
- *Is cheating a common theme in your family?*
- *Is gossip a common theme in your family?*
- *Is control over women the norm?*
- *What else is a common theme in your family?*

Now, before you want to leap through the book and punch me 🥊😄, please understand I'm just holding a mirror to what might be there. Even if you aren't dealing with some of these beasts in your family tree, you need to expect that the next generation will contend with them.

For example, in my family there was a financial cloud for many years. We constantly had money issues. While we accepted the pastoral BLESS-INGS and GIFTINGS, and accepted the blessing of discernment and social awareness, we had to confront the beasts of gossip, debt, unhealthy secrets, and addiction that run in my family. I'd found myself dealing with the same issues as previous generations.

My friend, it's time to acknowledge current reality and confront our beasts. You now hold the power to do something about them. And I'm going to be honest with you, I'm a little pissed off that I didn't know (and still don't know) all of my family blessings and all of my family beasts. None of it was in writing, or even conversations. There is still stuff I don't know, and probably never will. However, this is my declaration as a husband, father, coach, and as each and every one of your friend reading this: *this book is my manual to my next generation.* I will see to it that my kids have to fight less of my and my family's battles.

To Amaya, Kate, and Phoenix,

Please know this: our family has many generations of blessings that your

Mom and I have seen with our own eyes, have been made aware of, and have welcomed. They are as follows: abundance mindset, ministry (anointing), entrepreneur mindset, hard-work ethic, and genuine love for others.

Our family also has some things that, after spending much time in prayer, we have chosen to break with, no longer accepting them as "OK" or "normal."

These are things such as: addiction to alcohol and sexual issues, keeping secrets, divorce, financial debts and problems, unfaithfulness in marriage, pride, controlling, blaming and not taking personal responsibility.

We, as your Mom and Dad, have taken personal responsibility and chosen to make sure you and our family live and operate in freedom in all that I have listed above. Please know that as you get older and have more questions, no subject is off-limits. We can talk about any of it in great detail whenever you need to.

Wood Family Values: We take personal responsibility and never blame. We go where God calls us to be and not where income calls us to be. We judge no one and understand that everyone is on their own journey.

We love unconditionally.

Love,
Mom and Dad (Papa)

PASSING ON BLESSINGS

So, my friend, I'm totally aware there are things in your family lineage that are hard to accept. But there are also blessings of which to be proud. Either way, it's up to you what you and your family and generation will stand for. My challenge to you is to take time doing the exercise above. Find the good in what you can. Don't get hung up trying to change what you can't. And start planting the seeds to grow your family tree. Pass onto the next generation the blessings you're creating today.

WE MUST CHANGE OUR FAMILY TREES

Change your family legacy. Acknowledge what your family has done well and accept it. But let's not be naive about the crap that is in our family trees. If it's obvious that destructive behavior runs in our family, then we have two choices: we can either choose to ignore it, or accept it for what it is and do something about it. It's 100 percent up to us to take personal responsibility and no longer blame anyone.

It is time to break depression, lack of finances, multiple divorces, average thinking, average lives, anger, addiction, hurt, mental illness, a just-enough mindset, or whatever else poisons you every day. Even if no one but you knows you deal with it, YOU know it's crippling you on the inside. Know this. Your kids are depending on you to contend, fight, and clear the land of the generational crap so they can harvest breakthrough for generations to come.

"BECOMING A MILLIONAIRE STARTS WITH OUR MINDSET, NOT A NUMBER IN OUR BANK ACCOUNT."

—@THEREALDOUGWOOD

#CHURCHBOYTOMILLIONAIRE

CHAPTER SIX

MILLIONAIRE MINDSET

Church Boy to Millionaire, what does that even mean? I think we can make assumptions about what a church boy might be, but what does MILLIONAIRE mean to you?

Most people think it has to do with having at least $1,000,000 more in assets than in liabilities. Or we automatically make assumptions about how much is in our bank account 💰. Or maybe we've watched game shows on TV and it seems like a far-fetched dream that only the lucky few achieve. But what if I told you it has little to do with how much money is in your bank account, what your assets are, what your profit and loss statement says, or how much debt you have?

There are some people in this world who are millionaires on paper, but don't have a MILLIONAIRE MINDSET. You see, everything starts with a mindset that I like to call: abundance. If you have an abundance mindset you have a millionaire's mindset. And if you stay on this path, you may very soon be a millionaire on paper as well.

Abundance is a mindset that understands there are unlimited resources in this world. And anyone who chooses to accept total responsibility for their health, wealth, family, and influence, will find there is more than enough to go around!

Understand that ABUNDANCE isn't about the current status of your relationships, marriage, or physical health. It has nothing to do with the job you have, your relationships with your Creator or your church, or the music you listen to.

Abundance has 100 percent to do with YOU and YOUR mindset. On my journey from church boy to millionaire, I realized I was lacking abundance in key areas of my life. So, let's talk about creating abundance in your family, business, and relationships. What is an abundance mindset? Let's start with these questions:

- When someone says, "That person is successful," what does that mean to you?
- When someone says, "I go to a big church," what does that mean to you?
- When someone says, "I live in an average-sized city," what is that to you?
- When someone says, "My kids are well-behaved," what does that mean to you?
- When someone says, "I have an amazing marriage," what does that mean to you?
- When someone says, "They have a lot of money," how much money does that mean to you?

The list could go on. But the point is, I guarantee not one of our answers are the same. So the next question is, on what basis did you decide your answers? Probably on your results this far in life, your level of awareness as to what is out there, and your beliefs about what is possible.

BLAME, SHAME, AND WOE-IS-ME

I made a shift a few years ago in the way I looked at life. As I shared earlier, I spent a lot of time in blame, shame, and woe-is-me thinking. It's almost like the Disney character Eeyore, constantly saying things like: "I'm never lucky," "People like me never win the lottery," "Why did they get the promotion?" "Why do they have the big church?" "Why did they get blessed with musical talent?" "Why did they build their business so fast?" "Why are they always lucky?" "Why is their marriage so good?" "Why are they so thin?"

You know what? I realized this had 100 percent to do with my own mindset, the way I was raised, and what I was told by people I respected or were in authority. The problem is they were giving advice that was only half-true. *Some* of it was true, but some of it was limited by what they could see.

We adopt our parents' thinking, friends' thinking, pastors' thinking, and even our social media friends' thinking. Our results this far in life are an expression of our level of awareness, our surroundings, our friends, the books we've read (or haven't read), and the teachings we've chosen to believe.

LIVING ABOVE THE LINE

Here's the truth my friends, an abundance mindset starts by choosing to take PERSONAL RESPONSIBILITY and live a life ABOVE THE LINE. And what is an above-the-line mindset, Doug? Well, I'm glad you asked. It starts with taking personal responsibility.

ABOVE THE LINE	Personal responsibility, adds value to others, gratitude, goals, accountable, consistent, open-minded, coachable,	seeks solutions, owns mistakes, contender, abundance mindset, results-oriented, on purpose, massive action,	integrated life, socially aware, self-respect, desire for more, boundaries, congruent with spouse
BELOW THE LINE	Blames others, passive-aggressive, gossip, broke mindset, accepts debt as normal,	lives for the past, lives for judgment, cynical, victim mindset, controlling, constant drama, denial,	makes excuses, constant fear, blames spouse, complacent, emotionally unstable, no goals

Now that we've confronted our beasts, we've come to realize some of them came from people we love, respect, and care about. But, they have not served us well. Some of us have made agreements and accepted a word I believe should be a cuss word: *something called NORMAL.* And it's something we're looking at as below the line.

I'm sorry someone told you debt is normal. Or that $75,000–$150,000 per year is a lot of money. But if that's you, you are only one minor disaster away from complete financial mayhem. And most likely if you're reading this, you're dependent on one income to take care of your family. If you are not open to making a second, third, or fourth stream of income 💰, you will pay the price, unfortunately, very soon, or at least in the next five years.

Now let's pause for a second. You may be saying, "Doug, I'm doing well at $100,000 per year." Or, "I have a six-figure job." OK, but why do we think that's good? Well, because someone told us that $100,000 per year is good, because that's as big as we could see it, because we're not open to other ideas, because we're contracting rather than expanding, or maybe it's because we're not willing to be committed or misunderstood.

DOUGISM #8

ARE YOU WINNING AT LIFE, OR JUST ONLINE?

So many people are winning at fantasy football, games on their phone, poker, or how many likes or followers they have—but losing at REAL life. If your real life is winning, then by all means, play as many online games as you want. But if your family (or bank account) is suffering, then check your priorities!

So, looking at the table, what areas have you said are normal? My friends, life does not have to be normal. It's up to us to confront it and raise our standards.

THREE VIRUSES

Our abundance is constantly being blocked by three viruses: *us, our thinking, and our settling for average.* But honestly, I don't believe you made it this far in the book if that's really you. Thank you for choosing to play above the line in your legacy, for your family, and for your kids who need you to raise your standards. Not your standards of living (although I would love to see that for you also), but what I'm talking about here is your mindset for making a lasting impact spiritually, emotionally, financially, and physically. I think you know exactly what I'm talking about.

You see, it's often the people who have accepted "normal" that we allow to speak into us who keep our mindset below the line. We might go to church with them. We might be in small group with them each week, we most likely work with them. They may even be family. And I don't know about your friends, but Thea and I have had to make some hard decisions (more on this in Chapter 7).

In the last few years, we've had to ask who has an ABUNDANCE MINDSET and who doesn't? Because the people who don't are toxic and very soon I will start feeling comfortable around them. You may have heard it before, but we are most like (or soon will become like) the five people we spend the most time with. Another way of looking at it is, do I respect or desire the life they live? Would you want their bank account? Do you respect their marriage and the way they treat or talk about their spouse? Do you respect their morals, character, and integrity? These are just things to consider.

Now, I'm for the average person with an above-average desire to become the best version of themselves. I make no apologies, because I'm an average kid from an average small town in Forest Grove, Oregon. I went

to an average church and school. The only thing ABOVE average about me was my desire for more, but my debt and weight always held me down.

The truth is, God did not put us on this earth to be like everybody else and live the 40/40/40 plan. Work forty hours a week, for forty years, making $40,000 per year and then die on social *in*-security. Or even what use to be my case four years ago: the 80/80 plan. You know, the eighty-hour work week grind for $80,000 per year, and never having a life or getting to see your family because you're always WORKING.

My friend, God gave us gifts, talents, skills, abilities that can be even more developed, more unique, and serve others to be GREAT. But it takes ACTION. You have the skills within you right now, they just need some exercise. They just need to be dusted off. Start right now by making the decision to BE GREAT. Plant the seed of greatness in your mind. Grow YOURSELF! Remember, YOU are your greatest asset.

YOUR GOALS

How, you ask? Start with your goals.

- Write down the goal you will achieve one year from now (the one you know in your heart is overdue!).
- Now write down which goal you will need to achieve in six months to set you up for your one-year goal.
- Next, write down your 30-day goal to set you up for your six-month, and then one-year, goals.
- Now, bring it all the way down to what you need to do this week, and even today.

Now, dream a little with me. Where will you be one year from now? Or how about even one month from now?

Visualize it. Get with a mentor, a coach, your pastor, or someone that has done what you want to do. Then, be willing to have some truth spoken to you! It will help you accomplish what you desire to do. Then, ask for help to set an ACTION plan so you can work and make it happen. You were not meant to do life alone. The biggest mistake I see the people I coach make is they can see it, even know what they want, but are unwilling to take the CONSISTENT action it takes to accomplish the goal. That's why I always say, "Make the DAILY COMMITMENT to be CONSISTENT."

My friends, remember this: do not stop at anything (or for anyone) when you were already born GREAT. "People" cannot and don't have to understand YOUR dream, work ethic, your WHY, or why you flex your HUSTLE MUSCLE like you do 💪, because GOD did not give them your VISION!!! He gave it to you. Besides that, most people are OK with being OK.

Are you? Please tell me you are not. I'm sorry if someone got in your head and told you to chill out, or relax, or this is just the way it is. Blah, blah, blah . . .

You are God's greatest creation. YOU can do anything you want. And if for some strange reason you don't like where you're at, change it. We must stop this VICTIM mindset, thinking everyone is out to get us, and wondering why our break hasn't come. Really, we must get up and change our own channel. If we can scroll through social media everyday, then we can stop the madness of our personal life, accept personal responsibility, and choose to start living a life above the line. Plus, for you social media scrollers, it's not a healthy habit. We all know that too much scrolling just leads to minor depression and below-the-line thinking right?

God is trying to bless our socks off! Breakthrough, impact, raises, wealth, business ideas, ministry ideas, and so many more are trying to find us. Why are WE fighting it? I'll tell you why: Because we haven't raised our standards. We haven't taken full responsibility. We have not yet chosen to live above the line. So, before we go any further, draw a line on a piece of paper, in the sand if you are on a beach right now, or wherever else you might be, and choose to live a life ABOVE THE LINE.

ABUNDANCE STANDARDS

One of the ways we know we're living in ABUNDANCE, or the MILLIONAIRE MINDSET, is when we know that our coach, pastor, boss, team, church, partners, family, or whoever else is a RESOURCE for growth, and not an EXCUSE of why things are not changing.

The church we were raised in, the jobs we have, the promotion we missed, are all lessons and no longer excuses. Now, I know personally and fully believe that in order for blessing and breakthrough to come, we must raise our standards. This is the key difference between people who GROW and change their life, and the people who stay the same.

Let me get transparent here. In the last two years I've given more money in non-taxable charities than to tax-sheltered ones. I don't let tax benefits tell me where to give. God or seeing a need tells me where to give. My ABUNDANCE doesn't come with a donation slip!

I give to people often (even some of you reading this book), because when God speaks to me, I've made sure money isn't an issue and that I can give freely without ever having to check my bank account or check with my wife. This matters and is important to me because I can't tell you how many times in the past I've wanted to give and to help, but I couldn't, because of my empty wallet or my massive debt load. Eventually you get sick and tired of being broke and will do whatever it takes to create wealth, to stop putting your family through the misery of "just enough," or keeping them one minor emergency away from having to move back in with a family member!

A few years ago, Thea and I made a decision that we would stop asking for handouts, or checks, and instead we would start writing them. That is one of our abundance standards. What are yours? Have you decided that $50,000, $100,000, or even $1,000,000 in yearly income is all you want to make? If so, that's fine. But why is that? Usually the moment people start to get close to their goal they back off and settle into "Just enough" mindset because they let a number control how hard they will work. Most people are letting $50,000 per year keep them from $50,000 per month.

Recently, I was talking to someone who often worked three jobs. But, the problem was, as soon as two of them started going well, they quit the third! I kid you not. They had made up in their mind that they needed to make "X" amount per month. Regardless of whether that was working 30 hours or 60 per week. So they would start working 60 hours per week to make the income they needed to stay just over broke. The second they matched their goal of just over broke, they backed off the hours, therefore backing off the income, and the process repeated itself. This is because they set a standard of working *just hard enough* to get by. The truth is, suffering from just-enough-syndrome puts their family at huge risk. My suggestion for anyone in this place is to find a side hustle that creates residual income so you are not always trading your time for money.

It's very important to leverage your time so money is flowing to you at all hours of the day. Being perfectly honest, I was closed off to this years ago. And always remember, broke, skeptical, and overweight is a bad combination—and this was me for ten years. It's important to open up our minds to different ways of helping people, and it's OK to earn income from it. Years ago, the Network Marketing world was plagued by a few bad eggs who gave it a bad name. However, it is the best business model in the world for the average person to make a huge impact and an incredible income.

Now, what about your HEALTH standards? I hear people say all the time, "Weight on the scale doesn't define me." But let me tell you, I lost 65 pounds nine years ago. And you know what? Because it was the lowest number I'd seen on the scale since high school, it became good enough for me. I allowed that number to define my health standards. But it isn't my fighting weight anymore. So I'm working to get even better, because my standard of abundance keeps going higher. But no matter who you are, there is the danger of settling.

You see, my friends, I'm on this journey of abundance with you. And every day I stay on it, my ministry explodes, my connections with people improve, and massive favor and wealth pour into my life. Why? Because I constantly choose to LIVE above the line and EXPECT abundance. It's become a way of living.

Even though some days I feel a magnet trying to pull me back, I remember that magnet is actually the 97 percent of people around us choosing average, choosing to live below the line, choosing to let their standards be set by everyone around them.

Now, let's go even further. What about your standards of GIVING? It doesn't take a lot of money to bless someone. You can bless someone by shooting them a text message and letting them know you're thinking of them. Or what if someone spills their coffee next to you at Starbucks? Do you look away and act like you don't see it? Or do you put your stuff down, ask the barista for a rag, and clean it up with (or for) them?

Men, why do many of you pee on the toilet seat and not clean it up? First of all it's freaking rude and disrespectful to the next guy (or woman!) that uses the toilet. It's just disgusting, but clearly to about 75 percent of men this is OK. I know this because about 75 percent of the bathrooms I go to in public—*and yes even at my church*—there is pee on the seat and it's just rude.

This is an area right here that shows that how you do one thing is how you do most things. If you don't have an ABUNDANCE MINDSET then how the hell are you going to change your family, your finances, or make this world a better place?

IT'S TIME FOR A CLEANSE

It's time to unfollow people, fan pages, or trash pages. It's time to get rid of things in your newsfeed that are clearly distractions, that cause confusion, feelings of jealousy, or are filled with people stirring up drama and debates. You have no time for that! It only frustrates you and may even send you back to places you now have peace or healing in.

Now go do it. Click unfollow and they will never know that they don't show up in your feed. Protect you! YOU need YOU at your best. It's time to adopt a MILLIONAIRE MINDSET and it starts with who we see appearing in our social media feeds.

DO IT EVEN WHEN IT'S NOT YOUR JOB

Recently, my family and I went to Flagstaff, Arizona to do some business and play in the snow. There was a big truck in front of us on the interstate carrying a huge load of hay bales. Well, something went wrong and about five of the bales flew off the truck and onto the road, and cars had to swerve everywhere to avoid them.

Now, I was actually running late to an appointment. But, even though we were half a mile past the accident, we pulled to the side of the road and started backing up. I knew we needed to help.

I was dressed in nice, clean clothes, all prepared for the meeting to which we were running late, and hopped out of our blacked-out Escalade 😜. (Yes, I do drive a nice car and have no issues talking about it, because when you work hard and have the abundance mindset, you can drive a nice car and enjoy it without having to explain it to others.) So there I was, in the middle of Interstate 17, by myself, moving hay bales. Well I won't dramatize this, one other person did join in to help me. But as we dragged them off the road so people wouldn't hit them and die, the other gentleman next to me was cursing.

He asked, "What kind of 'effing idiots wouldn't pull over and help us move these hay bales? Someone could hit these and get killed!" He was right, but the truth was, those weren't his or my hay bales to deal with. But for someone with an abundance mindset it's about doing what needs to be done, even if it's a personal inconvenience.

Here's another example: If you're in coaching or sales (which if you aren't you should consider, by the way) what day of the month or the year do you hit your numbers? And not the company's numbers, but the ones you've set for yourself? The bottom line is, people with an abundance mindset lead themselves. They don't suffer from lack syndrome, just enough syndrome, or made-it-another-month syndrome. Why? Because that way of thinking becomes a way of living. It grows into a virus that infects their entire life.

Abundance means choosing to do EVERYTHING with excellence. It means taking out the trash when it's not your job. It means if you see a piece of trash on the ground in a public place, picking it up. It means raising your hand to volunteer when no one else will take the time. It means taking the road less traveled. It means if people around you are telling you to chill out and relax, getting the hell away from those people and understanding that they are toxic to you and your future.

ABUNDANCE means crushing a MULTI-MILLION dollar sales goal by MULTIPLE-MILLIONS of dollars! Abundance, men, means not peeing on the toilet seat and leaving it for someone else to clean up. Abundance is when you grab a towel to clean up the water you splashed on the mirror. It's YOUR water, not the bathroom's! It means serving a hundred people in your church with excellence without complaining or comparing, or looking for the next gig that would only serve your ego.

Abundance means tipping at least 20 percent at bare minimum 💵, and that's if they did a sucky job. Abundance is when you can tip 25–50 percent sometimes, or even 100 percent on occasion. Abundance means not cheating your own integrity, asking for a water cup, and instead putting lemonade or soda in it. Abundance is not eating half of your meal and then asking the waiter to take it off the bill.

Abundance starts with something small that will get bigger and bigger if you act and lead big.

ABUNDANCE IN OUR FAMILIES

Now, who sets the abundance standards in your family? I'll tell you, in the Wood household, we have some non-negotiable rules around abundance. My family knows, if the job needs to be done, we do it. If something needs to be done, we do it. And about seven years ago, Baby Kate was having a hard time learning this lesson. She kept dropping trash on the ground and leaving it there. I talked to her about this multiple times. I explained that we need to clear our table at coffee shops and restaurants.

One day, she tossed her straw wrapper on the ground and walked away. So I said, "Baby Kate, please pick it up. We don't litter." But the next day, guess what? She did it again!

So, I had her pick up that piece of trash again and knew it was time to teach her a lesson about littering that she would never forget, I got down on her level. I said, "Baby Kate, don't ever leave your trash, or anyone else's, behind. For the next twenty-four hours, until tomorrow at 12 o'clock, you will hold this piece of trash in your hand. You will not let it go. You will go to the bathroom with it, you will shower with it. You won't do anything without this piece of trash in your hand."

The point is, anytime you see her around today, she'll be clearing the tables, doing the dishes, and cleaning up trash, more quickly than anyone. Now, she is getting older, but still needs a little encouragement here and there. Overall, though, she has become proactive and has chosen to live and play above the line.

HOW TO ACHIEVE FUTURE BREAKTHROUGH

Here's the truth, for future breakthrough, we have to confront our beasts and deal with our past from an abundance mindset. Years ago, when I closed my furniture store, I still owed debts to many different creditors from whom I bought furniture. Now, before I go any further, I knew I owed them, regardless of whether or not my circumstances allowed me to pay them at the time.

Once I vacated my store, I had a few truckloads of odds-and-ends pieces of furniture, tools, office supplies, and everything you can imagine it

takes to run a large retail and warehouse furniture store. So, we proceeded with yard sales and put items on Craigslist, trying to rid ourselves of all this stuff and generate some cash. Now just so you know, I was living on unemployment. I didn't know what I was going to do next and still owed a lot of money to a lot of vendors (like $18,000). In addition, I had a ton of credit-card debt. But it was up to me to make these debts right to my vendors.

I'm talking about vendors like Martin Furniture out of California, who thought I had packed up and would never see me again (like most furniture stores when they close). Yes, they could track me down, but frankly, people like me didn't have any money when we closed our stores. This was happening more often than not in 2008 in the furniture industry. So, there I was, thirty years old, and I had just generated over (would you ever guess) $20,000 in cash from yard sales and selling stuff online.

So, I had a nice cash cushion I could use as I figured out what was next and lived off the state—because they would have had no clue about the cash. Or I could pay Martin Furniture the $18,000 I owed, clear my conscience and my name, knowing I answer to my own God and my own integrity. You see, if I didn't pay this money back, I would be putting my family, integrity, and future blessings at risk because I would be stealing it. And even though many around me say, "It's normal not to pay everyone back when going out of business," I still wrote the check.

One week later I get a call from the finance department of Martin Furniture. They literally called me shocked, and thanked me as they didn't know what to do or where to find me. Of course I had not changed my number ☺. However, I told them I answer to God, my character, and being an example of integrity and abundance to my kids, more than I answer to them. Honestly, the list of examples could go on, as I've had multiple chances to cheat on my taxes, also. But why would I ever put my future blessings at risk for a few bucks? Or a few thousand bucks? Or even a few million bucks?

Abundance is doing what's right NOW and in the moment, knowing that you will not risk the future blessings of your family tree. You see, even though I was broke as a joke back then, I had an abundance mindset and that's all I needed.

ABUNDANCE and INTEGRITY are similar, but they are different. Abundance is beyond morality. It's doing what you don't *technically* have to do. Was paying back my creditors a requirement? NO. I could have filed for bankruptcy and gotten out of it. That's normal. That's what the 97 percent do. That's how those with good-enough syndrome live. But that's the whole point.

Now, I'm not pointing fingers at anyone who's filed for bankruptcy. But my family did not go out to eat and we didn't sip on lattes. During this time, I looked my girls in the eyes and said, "Mommy and Papa owe some people money. So, we're going to do what's right and pay them back, even though we don't have to."

You see, integrity is doing the right thing, it's doing what's expected of you with or without anyone looking. But I'm talking about abundance. And abundance is about leading yourself regardless of what's expected!

ABUNDANCE ATTRACTS ABUNDANCE

Abundance is an attractive quality. You will attract amazing people when you choose to live a life of abundance. And how do abundant people act? Well, I could list many people who know my income (or at least assume it), but still try to pick up the tab when we're out for dinner. And anyone who knows me understands that I will fight for the check when it's time to pay! But it's the effort that's impressive.

There is nothing worse than the guy or gal who has the puppy-dog look on their face when the check comes. Or for some reason expects you to pay. No one likes to be around this person and they won't ever get invited to dinner again. This is a cling-on and they have a habitual broken mindset.

Also, when someone picks up your check, regardless of whether you put up a fight or not, you had better say a great big THANK YOU. Don't let pride get in the way. It's ugly. And a quick note to the ballers and shot callers out there who usually pick up the tab—*by the way I respect these people*—it's important to allow someone else to pick up the tab once in awhile if they really want to or try 😎.

I've also learned to live in the thankful zone as well, and letting them grab the check for you is a new way for them to step into abundance, and to live in a better place as God is probably working abundance into their heart. Plus, they sometimes need bragging rights saying they beat you to the check. Let them have a win once in awhile ☺.

Here's how abundant people don't live. When the check comes, don't pat your pockets and say you forgot your wallet. Don't mysteriously take a bathroom break when it's time to pay the tab. You see, abundance bosses up. Understand this, if you're not living in abundance, don't get disappointed when you aren't invited to things.

People who choose to live below the line won't stay hanging out with those who choose to live above it. There's an incongruence there. And you must be congruent with abundant people to hang with them.

Abundant people talk differently, too. Is the word struggle a key part of your vocabulary? If so, cut it out. Don't overuse it. It magnifies the problem and steals your power at creating solutions. Instead, start using the word "CONTENDING." This means you are taking the power to overcome. Instead of struggling to survive, you're contending for breakthrough! When you make this change, watch what happens.

- Struggling with health? No, you're contending for health!
- Struggling in finances? No, you're contending for healthy finances!
- Struggling in your marriage? No, you're contending for a thriving marriage!
- Struggling in school? No, you're contending for your degree!
- Struggling with your coworkers? No, you're contending for healthy relationships at work!
- Struggling with your doctor's diagnosis? No, you're contending for a miracle!

Remember my friends, you are God's highest creation. You are not struggling. Don't give your challenges so much power over you. You are abundant, strong, and made for more. It's time to step up, to contend for breakthrough for yourself, your business, your ministry, your family, and for everything that matters most. It's time to contend for a millionaire mindset. And when you do, you'll unlock blessing for thousands because you stepped into it.

DOUG, WHAT DOES IT TAKE?

———

Answer: as long as your faith and family are in order, then it usually takes more than you are doing right now. Here are a few things to consider 👍. It takes . . .

- ✅ Less TV and more action
- ✅ Less excuses and more structure
- ✅ Less "chill out friends" and more PURPOSE friends
- ✅ Less scrolling and more reading
- ✅ Less caring what others think and more of caring what YOU think
- ✅ Less music and more podcasts
- ✅ Less happy hour and more work
- ✅ Less trying to sell and more trying to give
- ✅ Less perfectionism and more authenticity
- ✅ Less strategy and more passion and heart 🤍
- ✅ Less telling and more listening
- ✅ Less ideas and more implementation
- ✅ Less randomness and more consistency
- ✅ Less about you and more about others
- ✅ Less downtime and more purpose time
- ✅ Less convenience and more commitment

Abundance is a mindset, not a bank account.

"GROWTH AND HAPPEN RESULTS WHEN YOU ARE WILLING TO BE MISUNDERSTOOD."

CHAPTER SEVEN

WHY OUR FRIENDS HOLD US UP

It's important that you understand something about my life, and the purpose of this book. I have made some very key decisions that were complete PATTERN DISRUPTIONS for myself, my family, and the people around me. They were hard to do. Before you go any further, understand: this book is about leveling up, and to do so, you'll need to experience pattern disruptions, too.

You will be going to new places—mainly in your mindset. Why? Because our mindsets are the things holding us up; they lead to our BEHAVIORS, and our behaviors produce our RESULTS. So, we will also take a deep dive into the behaviors that keep us stuck in just-enough syndrome—at least they did for me.

You see, broke behaviors keep us operating below the line. And leveling up is how we change our results for ourselves and our families. Now, what is LEVELING UP? It's choosing to get away from broke. It's choosing to stop settling. It's choosing to do hard things. It's acknowledging what we're doing, and the way we're operating, isn't working anymore.

The wrong day-to-day behaviors are ruining us. And our current mindsets must change. Now, let me share where these changed the most in my life: *by disrupting unhelpful patterns*.

ARE YOUR FRIENDS KEEPING YOU FROM BREAKTHROUGH?

Here's something that often surprises people: our current friends, or even family, are usually keeping us from BREAKTHROUGH. When we are leveling up, we start speaking a different language. Our words change, and so do our actions. We become different, and people notice. We don't connect with others in the same ways we once did—almost like a cell phone with an upgraded signal. It can't communicate as well (or at all) with the *old* frequencies it used to. Another way to put it is there is a below-the-line frequency, and an above-the-line frequency. This creates a disconnect.

For example, have you ever gotten a text from someone and immediately thought, "Ugh, I'll get back to them later." It takes effort and calories to communicate with them. We put off returning their text or call as long as possible. This is one of the small ways we can know we're on different frequencies. On the other hand, there are people who text or call us we immediately respond to. They don't drain us. You are each tuned to the same frequency.

Several years back, Thea and I experienced this same thing while living in Oregon. We were starting another business, and we were already in the middle of a lot of transition. We tried a few different churches in our hometown, and finally found a church home that we loved. We lead a small group. We helped with announcements. And we would even speak at the seasonal banquets.

Our business was growing successfully and we were able to help a lot of people that attended the church through it. Every Sunday, we had people thanking us. They would stop us in the foyer and say, "Thank you for all you have done in helping me change my life!"

However, this was also when things started to get . . . weird. Thea and I would fly off every couple of months to conferences where we learned to become better. We were confronting our beasts, growing in EMOTIONAL INTELLIGENCE, improving our COMMUNICATION SKILLS, and becoming more authentic leaders. Then, we'd come back home, show up to church on Sundays like always—but things were starting to feel different. Like I said before, it was getting awkward.

I was in church one Sunday morning, and something the pastor said (as he gave his opinion) sounded like a swipe at the business I was a part of. But, as I had learned in one of my personal growth conferences and the great book "The Four Agreements," I didn't make assumptions and decided not to take it personally. I chose to think the best and didn't say anything to anyone.

Over the next few weeks, people continued thanking us for the value we offered on social media. We posted encouraging videos about leadership, health, business, and even God. Sometimes these conversations took place in front of people, and other times in private. But Thea and I had chosen to share truth with people through social media, so that's what we kept doing.

A few weeks later, the pastor was sharing a great message—but for some reason, things felt even more off. He'd said something that, in my mind, could have needlessly offended many in the audience. It had nothing to do with me, my business, or the Bible—they were comments about culture. So, I messaged my friend who used to be a part of the church to ask about it. He was someone whom I trusted and respected and had also attended the church before moving away.

I explained what the pastor said. Then I asked, "Does this sound like something he would've said or spoken when you were here?"

He replied, "Ha! Oh yeah. That's just his personality!"

I thought to myself, "What's changed?"

I spent a few more weeks asking myself that question about our church and our pastor. He is a man I had respected and he had helped me so much through the years. But still, things were feeling more and more off.

Then it hit me like a ton of bricks: *nothing had changed, I had changed.*

My friends, that is the first time I realized that when you're pursuing growth, there are good people, wealthy people, Godly people, often even family, co-workers, or gifted communicators you may be surrounded by that are great, but they're not moving. You are leveling up, but they're staying the same. And I'm telling you, you will have to identify your patterns— who and where you're spending most of your time—and confirm people around you are on the same path.

Let me say this. You aren't weird for having thoughts like mine! There's nothing wrong with you, and you don't have to justify them. People may be telling you that what now feels off to you is totally normal. But there's a voice inside of you crying out that nothing feels normal anymore.

THE NEW NORMAL

My friends, this is how you know you're on the path to complete breakthrough for you, your family, and your legacy. But now it's up to you to do something about it. Take these situations, for example:

- The guys you're watching the game with, the conversation's not the same anymore, is it?
- The guys in your fantasy football league, it's just not the same anymore, is it?
- The people in your bowling league are cool, but it's just different, isn't it?
- For some of you, it may be showing up at your church on Sunday mornings like always, and even though everything appears the same, something or some people are different, aren't they?
- You spend Thanksgiving dinner and birthday parties with the same family and the same friends, but again, something's missing, isn't it?
- The people you vacation with, boat with, or barbeque with just don't feel the same, do they?

My friends, YOU are growing. YOU have chosen to live at a higher level, and you're in the process of leveling up. Here's the truth, for growth to happen, you must choose to disrupt your pattern. Let me be clear. I'm not saying you HAVE to leave or make changes regarding anything I've just said. But, YOU will need to CHOOSE who and where you spend your time. Whatever and whoever you are around is feeding you something. Just make sure you're eating what your future self needs.

DOUGISM #11

DRAMA-FREE ZONE

Establish a DRAMA-FREE ZONE. Don't put up with negativity or drama from anyone; this includes family. This must become a non-negotiable. Some people need drama like I need oxygen. But the only way to starve drama is by leaving it alone, not responding to it, or not engaging with it. And never, for any reason, deal with passive-aggressive or compulsive people who engage in this behavior. You must create a drama-free zone around you.

P.S. If drama keeps surrounding you, then quickly do a pulse check! Is it you?

Massive growth doesn't come from lateral moves. It comes from taking a stand for something great, for your best self, for being willing to be misunderstood, and even a willingness to be lonely for a while.

Why? Because the process of PATTERN DISRUPTION is lonely.

There simply aren't as many people choosing to leave the comfort of their routines, and live life weirdly. I don't want to be normal. Normal is broken. Normal is where I lived for the first thirty-five years of my life. Let's face it, I'm weird. But I've never experienced so much freedom as I have by disrupting key patterns in my life.

IDENTIFYING AREAS NO LONGER SERVING YOU

What are areas you may need to disrupt that are no longer serving you? We like the comfort of our routines. You know, the routines we repeat the same week over and over again, the same month over and over again, and the same year over and over again.

Now, these patterns actually help us navigate and protect us from the unknown. But the truth is, we're unconscious of how our patterns are keeping us trapped. Some of them hold us back from being all we can be.

So, what patterns used to serve you well that aren't helping anymore? What patterns are you comfortable with, that you once loved and enjoyed, that aren't feeling like they once did? Understand, patterns are neither good or bad, they just are. There are patterns that simply stop working because we have changed and they no longer serve us. They can be people, places, things, or beliefs. Remember patterns are not good nor bad, they just are. It's just as important to acknowledge them.

Here's what they may start feeling like:

- *They are empty and unfulfilling.*
- *They aren't working for you anymore.*

- *They are confining, constricting, and limiting.*
- *You're starting to wonder if there's more.*
- *They leave you with unfinished work.*
- *You feel like you can't pretend anymore.*
- *You have changed, but things around you have not.*
- *Or you simply don't see things the way you used to anymore.*

Here is who or what these patterns might involve:

- *Your workplace*
- *Your friendships*
- *Your family and traditions*
- *A best friend you used to share everything with*
- *A particular church (or religion)*
- *Holidays and who you want to spend them with*
- *Traditional vacation friends*
- *Or even a mentor, coach, or someone you hold in high respect*

Now, I want to be crystal clear, all of these people, places, or things are probably very good in and of themselves. They haven't changed—but you have. So now we have to choose: are we going to do something about it?

For the record, I'll say it one more time. You don't have to do anything about any of it. But understand, as long as you're leveling up, these feelings aren't going away. They are not going to feel normal again.

WHAT TO DO ABOUT IT

Thea and I were in this exact place. We identified unhelpful patterns, and needed to disrupt them. This meant we had to have some hard conversations with a few family members about the holidays. They needed to look different. We did choose to find a church that was aligned with the future we wanted to create.

We realized we were sending our girls to a religious institution that was moonlighting as a good school with good character, but the truth was, it

was preparing them for a world that was relevant thirty years ago (like much of the education system today!). So, we're no longer participating in it. We recognized patterns in our girls' schooling we didn't like and chose to find a partner and create an online school that was willing to disrupt those patterns and redesign education. It's called Valor Global Online (ValorGlobalOnline.org). Check it out 😎.

This may sound brutal, but we even discontinued some friendships and distanced ourselves from people with whom we used to vacation. Why? Because we weren't on the same frequency any longer. And truthfully, they had no desire to level up alongside us.

So, please understand this. As you disrupt patterns in your life, it's normal for people to get uncomfortable with you. It's just how it goes. They may not like it. They might start talking about you behind your back. But your job from this day forward, if you are committed to this, is to set you, your family, and your legacy up to win—NOT to live to make those around you feel comfortable.

If you do this, expect problems. You don't have to tell people the whole truth. You don't owe them an explanation. Just do you. You may need to just simply change the conversation around why you aren't celebrating a certain holiday with them like you do every year. Here's the truth, you owe ZERO people an explanation for identifying patterns to DISRUPT in your own life. Remember, they did nothing wrong. You are just choosing to get better. But this will ruffle their feathers. Be prepared. So just make sure you are 100 percent committed to it because it will not be easy with some people. Either way it will be hard. Choose your hard!

WHAT WILL YOU DISRUPT?

So my friends, what patterns do you need to disrupt? Take action now. Have the conversation with your spouse, call a family meeting, and get serious about it. Because nothing will change until you take action. The power is in the choices we make. We can continue to react to circumstances in our life, or we can create the life we want. Our life is a canvas and we are the painters.

I promise, when you do this, here's what you'll see. When we sit with the winners, the conversation is different. People often message me and say, "Wow, Doug, it seems like the crew you roll with are cut from a different cloth. They seem to be thriving and having a lot of fun in life."

Well the answer is YES!!! But know that we understand we're all *still becoming* who we want to be. We have all come from average lives, averages churches, small towns, and lives of normal. And truthfully, if it wasn't for someone else LIVING a life that shows there is so much more that's possible—we wouldn't be THRIVING.

We are just average people finding our paths to make above-average lives for ourselves and our families. But I will say this, when you sit with those winners, and those who are thriving, there will be some side effects. You will most likely get healthier, your income will go up, and you will level up in every area of life.

Someone just said to me again yesterday, "Doug, since I have been talking to you lately and applying your coaching to my life, my marriage and my income have gotten better." I know. I have this impact on those who are ready to change. If you follow what is laid out in this book and hang around people who are doing this too, you will thrive as well. It's the simple TRUTH.

STOP CARING WHAT OTHERS THINK

Now, let me end it with this. You will draw criticism, negative comments, and people who feel the need to talk behind your back. Why? Because leveling up makes the people around who don't want to grow uncomfortable.

Aunt Bonnie, Pastor Bill, cousin Larry, your former best friend Gina, or that one friend you hung out with for a few summers weren't given your dream or your purpose. Unless they are going to pay your mortgage next month, they have ZERO RIGHT to tell you how to live, what to do (or not do), what business you can start or be a part of, or what to post on your social media pages. These people are toxic in the worst way.

Just because they may have given up on their dreams, have bought into average thinking, are broke, or skeptical, fear your growth as a person, don't like that you hang out with other people, feel insecure that you're taking your health to the next level, or they choose to spend energy in negativity and judgement, doesn't mean they get to pull you down. Get 100 percent focused on YOU and what YOU are about. And I guarantee, compulsive worry about what others think of you will stop. I realized a while ago that I can't pay my bills with other people's opinions of me!

The truth is, what got you where you are today won't get you to where you want to go. And your ability to grow into your best self is almost 100 percent connected to WHO you start spending most of your time with. Who you spend your time with is who you will become. And the wrong group of people with the wrong habits pull us down more quickly than anything.

Once you have tasted GREATNESS and are in the IN-BETWEEN stage of confronting your beast and adopting that millionaire mindset, there are people from which you must protect yourself. It's very IMPORTANT that at this point of your journey you spend more than two-thirds of your time with people who are at your growth level (or higher) or are at least on the same mission. Remember, when you sit with the winners—the conversation is different—and soon you will be different too.

Spend more time with these people, even if it's through personal development books, podcasts, or video conferencing. Your online and on-purpose community might become your only community for a while. But that's okay.

Yes, this growth process will seem lonely at times. Keep moving forward and new friends will come. You will attract higher quality people into your life as you level up, because you are where they are and are going where they want to go.

Now, what patterns will you disrupt to level up?

DOUGISM #12

BE READY FOR PUSHBACK

Be prepared. Anytime you start to move, challenge the *status quo*, or start to grow, there will be major pushback from the people in your closest circles. Decide on the front-end who's going and who's growing. Don't ever apologize for your growth!

"TODAY'S LEADERS ARE USING INNOVATIVE TECHNOLOGY AND ARE ENGAGED ON SOCIAL MEDIA TO GROW THEIR ORGANIZATIONS."

—@THEREALDOUGWOOD

CHAPTER EIGHT

ONLY TAKE ADVICE FROM WINNERS

My friends, don't let your ego get in the way before you figure this out: *you can accomplish anything faster by learning from someone who has already done it successfully.* If you want to be a millionaire, get around millionaires. If you want to start a business, then seek advice from someone who has started a successful business. If you want to start a non-profit,  then find someone who has done it successfully. If you want to be a better speaker, go learn from a good speaker.

Here's the truth, in this day and age you will get run over if you try to do everything on your own. I needed help writing this book, I needed someone to help me outline and get in my head to help my external process and type for me. So, I found someone who was skilled in this.

I'm absolutely baffled that people are so freakin' stubborn and try to do everything on their own and then end up doing nothing. And when you ask them whatever they told you they were going to do, you can tell they are manufacturing some lame excuse for why the project hasn't moved an inch. But they're still trying to act like it has. I just call it straight up B.S. Remember, your ego is not your amigo. Want to do something great? Get around the greats, or better yet, find someone to assist you so you stay in your unique ability and they stay in theirs.

Thea and I use the phrase "better together." We're always better working with others than we are when trying to do life alone. Now please, hear my heart. I respect anyone trying to start something. But trying to do everything on your own will hold you up.

Stop trying to do everything on your own. Get advice from pros and find someone, people, or a group to partner with. I see this all the time with people trying to lose weight. They diet in secret and because they don't know what to do and are tired of failing, it's easier to stay alone out of fear of failure or accountability. Someone was bragging to me the other day about how they are so healthy, how my program won't work for them, and they only eat "Paleo." And I was like, yeah, I can tell. (To myself I was saying, "Clearly too much Paleo ☺.") I know that's kind of intense, but it's true. This person does have a portion-control problem, but the real issue is this person needs a guide or coach to assist them. And they just need to ask for help to get some wins.

WHO'S IN YOUR TRUTH CORNER

However, be careful who you get your advice, prayer, and council from. Have you heard of the AMEN corner? It's filled with the people who cheer you on no matter what, who pat you on the back and say, "Good job!" But I want to ask you, who's in your TRUTH corner? They will most likely be the people willing to call you on your B.S. when you're out of line.

The scariest place to be is around people who always agree with you, or who always go along with whatever you say, or are scared to tell you the TRUTH because of how you will react or treat them.

I call the people you pick for your truth corner the Wise Counselors. They will always meet four standards:

1. *Have they done what you're trying to do?*
2. *Were they successful at it?*
3. *Are they still doing it?*
4. *Will they be threatened by your success?*

HAVE THEY DONE IT?

The first thing you're looking for in a Wise Counselor is whether or not they've done what you're trying to do. For example, if you want to start a church, this person better have done this successfully (by your definition). If you want to start a podcast, and are asking your mentor who has never done—or even listened to—a podcast, they're not a Wise Counselor in this area because they have not successfully done it.

If you want to start an orphanage in Africa, and you're getting advice from your dad who's only been on one mission trip, you'll want to talk to someone besides your dad. Before you get all feisty with me, I know your dad's a great, integrous guy, and successful businessman, but if he hasn't done it, talk to someone who has. The point is, get around a Wise Counselor who has done it successfully.

WERE THEY SUCCESSFUL?

A Wise Counselor is also someone who has done what you're trying to do—and was SUCCESSFUL. But PLEASE understand I'm not talking about perfection! I'm talking about people who are in the game and have done (or at least attempted) what you want to do.

If you're getting marriage advice from someone with three failed marriages, watch out. I'd say you need to get advice from someone with a thriving marriage. If you want to start a church, get advice from someone who's started a church from scratch that is STILL thriving and growing five years or more later. If you want to write a book, are you talking to successful authors? If you want to get physically healthy, are you talking to someone who's gotten healthy recently? Or who has helped a lot of other people do so?

Now, you might be saying, "But Doug, successful people are really busy. How will they have any time to talk with me?"

Here's what you don't know. Everyone messages me and says, "Doug I know how busy you are . . . ." Interesting, because I didn't know they could see my calendar, unless you can see someone's calendar—*which you can't*— you don't know if someone is actually busy or not! For example, someone flew into Scottsdale recently on a family vacation. He messaged me before-hand, saying, "Hey Doug, I know we've only met once, but I respect you and what you've done so much. I know you're probably busy, but could you meet me for coffee?"

Remember, never assume someone is busy. Because here's why, the squeaky wheel gets the grease. I didn't see that message for a couple days because it went to spam. So, another message popped in. Then I realized there were two more messages from this guy.

"Doug, will you meet me for coffee?"

"Hi Doug, I know you're really busy, but can you meet for coffee?"

Guess what, he was wrong. I wasn't too busy. I found out who he was legit. So I met him for coffee. I make time for people who are hungry when I have time or choose to make time, if they have a desire for more, and are coachable and teachable, then I do my best to assist.

So there we were the next day, drinking coffee (which he tried to buy). He brought a notebook, had pen and paper in hand, and came prepared with a list of ten questions. I gave him an hour-and-a-half of my time. Honestly, I didn't want to end the conversation, but we had to go!

The point is, when you sit with the WINNERS, the conversation is different. Want to be successful or even a MILLIONAIRE? Start hanging out with them, start picking their brain, start buying their books, listening to their podcasts, going to their conferences, if you can. Start drinking coffee with them. But here's a problem, you don't always know what they look like! The REAL successful people, or MISSIONAL MILLIONAIRES, don't flaunt their success—but you know enough to see success. They're the people who are constantly leveling up, and operating at a higher FREQUENCY. Getting on their frequency is important, because they are the Wise Counselors who can share their wisdom with you, or lead you to it.

ARE THEY STILL DOING IT?

Understand, we're living in a world in which technology and communication, are moving at an accelerated rate. Things are changing every six months to a year (AND WILL ONLY GET FASTER!!!). So, here's the truth, IF someone did something five, ten, or even twenty years ago, it's most likely outdated and irrelevant.

If someone is talking about the good ole' days, run as fast as you can. That's a has-been leader. Also, if you are getting advice from someone who is dogging technology, and wishing social media would just go away, or saying "how it used to be done," then you're hosed 😬.

Today's leaders are still actively in the game, on the front lines. They are using current technology, they are innovative. They are on and using social media to GROW their organization, and they're still producing at a fast pace and encouraging you to do it also. They are in the game, and encouraging you to break into new ways to grow and make a great IMPACT.

WILL THEY BE THREATENED BY YOUR SUCCESS?

Now my friends, last but not least—and this is hard to say—but pay attention to the people who aren't clapping when you succeed. You may be in a position in which someone you once sought advice from is now going through a season of challenge, pain, or hurt.

Unfortunately, even I have felt threatened by people that I've seen growing. There have been people I used to give advice to, mentor, or coach who were hard for me to watch succeed. I was happy on the inside for them—but there was a part of me that was jealous. I'll say, there may be people who aren't rooting against you, but are no longer rooting for you. Why? Because they feel insignificant or insecure. However, it is our responsibility to be considerate of these people. It's very important we do honor where someone came from, or may have started, otherwise we and others will forget the work and sacrifice it took to get things to where they ended up. Yes it's true, someone before us did walk uphill both ways in the snow. And that is why we can do the many great things we can do today.

Having said that, be careful. Don't constantly look for someone who is not supporting you—but please don't be surprised if Thanksgiving dinner just isn't tasting the same. If the barbeque with the same old group doesn't feel the same. If going to coffee with that same leader, boss, or pastor just doesn't have the same feeling to it. You know, you're not leaving conversations with them as encouraged or supported as you used to. Or maybe there are even areas of conversation you must avoid, or not talk about with that person or group.

If so, take these as signs you are leveling up, disrupted old patterns, and are growing. While it isn't your place to figure out or judge where they are at, it is your place to be aware, protect your dream, and continue creating your best self. Even if it's lonely for awhile, get around people who are clapping for and with you. Better yet, YOU clap for them and do it often. Because after all, what people like more than sex and money is recognition ☺.

So, let's give it to them.

DON'T BE AN ASK-HOLE

I will close with this. There is nothing—and I mean NOTHING—that I hate more than when someone I'm in a coaching relationship with becomes argumentative, disrespectful, or even does the exact opposite of what I suggest. I'm not saying you have to take all the advice you get—but my suggestion is: *don't be an ask-hole!*

What's an ask-hole 😝? An ask-hole is someone who asks you a question, and then does the exact opposite of what you suggested!

Here's the truth. People who ask me for advice and are then argumentative, disrespectful, or close-minded don't ever get time or conversation with me, and they can count on never getting open, honest, and truthful advice from me ever again. Why? Well I don't waste my time with know-it-alls and egos, because I don't want to get my head bitten off!

The bottom line, my friends, is to make sure you build a truth corner, not just an amen corner, and fill it with people who love you unconditionally. Get around people who will tell you if you're heading for a cliff. No matter how great you think things are going, Wise Counselors tell you the truth—and you will trust it.

Seek Wise Counsel or a coach who has done what you want to do, was successful at it, is still doing it, and won't be threatened by your SUCCESS. Oh . . . and one more thing . . . don't be an ask-hole 🙊!

KNOW YOUR WORTH

———

Distance yourself from people who disrespect you. Absolutely NO ONE should ever DISRESPECT YOU! Depending on the situation, put your foot down or ignore them. And if it happens again, DELETE them from your LIFE! You are worth too much to be disrespected.

"**BROKE, SKEPTICAL, AND OVERWEIGHT IS A** BAD COMBINATION."

—@THEREALDOUGWOOD

CHAPTER NINE

WHY COMFORTABLE PEOPLE STAY BROKE

Parents, let's start with us. We need to make sure we tell our kids "Yes," "Good job," and "Keep it up, baby!" as much as we tell them "No, we can't afford that" or "No, I don't have time." We must reinforce what's good. Many of us grew up hearing no constantly. And no wonder we don't have any money—we were told we couldn't afford things our whole lives! Let's not do this to our kids.

I mean this, be careful what you say no to, or you may just continue on the same broke journey. I think we all have a horrible habit of saying no too soon *and* too often. Because, let's face it, from a young age we're told no constantly. Now, I myself have had a tendency to say no too often. But I've realized every time I've said no too quickly, I've missed out on opportunities.

Looking back on my life, there were five blatant times I was dead wrong. And even though it took awhile to get it through my thick skull, I'm thankful I finally said yes. Had I not said yes, probably the five biggest blessings and breakthroughs in my life would not have happened.

LEAVING COMFORT BEHIND

The first situation happened in the summer of 1997. I had just gradu-ated high school and was now deciding what to do next. I could go to college like everyone else. But, deep inside I knew college wasn't right, as

I had never been a serious student. I could stay at home, continue working at the local pizza parlor, and stay close to my girlfriend at the time. Or I could go to a ministry training program in Phoenix, Arizona that, honestly, would be the best thing for me.

I knew if I went to college it'd be fun to party and hang out with my friends. I knew working at the pizza parlor would be easy because I'd keep the comfort of my routines and girlfriend at the time. But there was part of me that wanted to step out and get away—and something was telling me I should go to this ministry school in Phoenix. But still, I closed the door on this opportunity and settled into working at the pizza shop in Forest Grove. That was easier.

My parents nudged me left and right to go to Arizona. But, had it not been for Junior Siliga, now a good friend and mentor, I would've stayed boxing pizzas. You see, he had reached out to me a year prior and saw a struggling high school kid who just needed someone to talk to.

I had made up my mind not to go, but the day before the ministry school started, Junior called me. And he asked me to come all the way from Oregon to Arizona to go. Everything in me wanted to—*and tried to*—say no. But for some reason I couldn't. And the next day, I was on my way to Arizona with a car full of clothes, scared out of my mind, but knowing it was best for me.

Those two years in Master's Commission helped shape who I am today. Was the program perfect? No. Is any?! But did I finally understand who God was and what he could do through me? Yes. Looking back, if I would have stayed in Oregon I would most likely have never left. And just as important, had I said NO, I would not have met my wife, Thea.

DOUGISM #14

#SHIFTHAPPENS

Each time you become aware you're just going through the motions, it is a signal that it's time to shift, make a move, move on, or make a drastic change in your daily routine or your life. Allow the shift to happen, or make the shift happen! Otherwise, the same ole' shift will keep repeating itself.

GIVING EVERYTHING WE HAD

Thea and I had been married a few years. And each year we attended the "Breakthrough Conference" put on by a local church in Portland called City Bible. We went with an expectant heart, praying for new vision, and this year in particular, a breakthrough for our marriage, business, and what the future might hold as we were pretty much holding on by a thread in every area.

During the conference, there were three opportunities to give financially, investing both in the local church and in what financial blessings God may open up in our lives. See, you can think what you want about churches who ask for money, but on that particular weekend, the financial strongholds that had plagued generations of our family before us were broken.

Thea and I decided we would wait until the last night to give a donation, believing that God would do something with it for others and us as well. See, we had just refinanced our house and gotten a payout of $20,000. Because we were so strapped financially, the money would allow us and our company some breathing room for a few months. The night we were going to give, Thea and I decided we would both write a number on a piece of paper. If it was the same number, and we both felt comfortable with it, we'd write a check and give.

I wrote my number. She wrote hers. Then we showed each other. At first glance they looked the same—but then I looked again as if I was in a dream, or nightmare, and probably both. I, Mr. Financial Guy who knew what a mess we were really in, wrote $1,200. Thea, our dreamer and faith builder, wrote down $12,000. She had an extra zero 😫!

If looks could kill, Thea would not be breathing 😡. While Thea and I were in the most intense facial-expression argument ever, where your eyes are dropping F-bombs far worse than could ever come out of your mouth 😖, everyone around us were singing and enjoying the service. We waited until the end. I was the holdout—Thea was the dreamer. I was scared out of my mind and literally wanted to throw up. But I knew this money

wasn't just about the church or
the conference and had nothing
to do with Benny Perez taking
up a good offering. This was an
opportunity for us to let go of
what we thought was ours, but
actually wasn't.

We were (and still are) just a
conduit of what's been given to
us. If we wanted financial break-
through, we knew this was the process we had to take, regardless of whether
or not we'd get something back. I thank Benny Perez and City Bible Church
for giving us this opportunity that night. The financial burden that had
plagued my family for years had just been broken in the spirit realm.

After I finally came around, my eyes weren't steaming mad anymore.
And I said if we're going to give this check, we need to go ask for prayer,
because now we really needed a miracle 😱 ! You see, we'd already spent
$8,000 of our refinance money paying off a little debt, meaning $12,000
was EVERYTHING we had left.

We went to the front and asked for prayer. But something so unique
happened while they were praying for us. I felt everything they were saying
and praying was right. Until one guy said something that made no sense
at all.

He said, "Doug, very soon there will come a time where you will no
longer go to the refrigerator for comfort."

Wait, was this dude calling me fat 😳?!

He continued, "In fact, I believe God is birthing a ministry in you
to help others experience breakthrough in their financial and physical
health."

I'm thinking to myself, is this dude freaking nuts? I'm the fattest I've ever been. And now that I'm giving this $12,000, I'm broke, stupid, and even more in debt. AND I just refinanced my house to do this?!

You see nothing changed for a couple years in our financial situation. But something had changed. Letting go of MY money was actually letting go

of the pride. You see, when people who don't have any money hold onto it so tightly, it robs them of the freedom that there's so much of it out there, and there are blessings waiting to take place.

I realized, that weekend the Wood family snapped the debt chain that hung over our family. If I had said no, maybe we never would have.

HELPING THOUSANDS TRANSFORM

So, you've got to understand me. For many years I was the king of being broke and skeptical about anything and everything. Thea would sometimes come home and her friends were selling lotions, potions, or fancy energy drinks they wanted us to buy or try. I literally laughed at them and said, "If it's so good, they'd be selling them in the grocery store!"

Never forget, BROKE, SKEPTICAL, and OVERWEIGHT is a bad combination. My ego told me the only way to make money was either to work for someone or own a (traditional) business. But what is "traditional" anyway? To work the way people did ten or twenty years ago? Yeah how's that working out for everyone? It didn't work out well for me.

So there I was, broke, skeptical, and the heaviest I'd ever been. But still, I knew I finally needed to make a change. So, I started a HEALTH JOURNEY

and called a friend who had successfully lost weight and stayed
consistent with it (a Wise Counselor and coach). He suggested
I become a coach. But I said I
didn't have time, so he should
go talk to Thea. So she started to
coach.

The next thing you know,
she's having more fun, is more
fulfilled, and is enjoying a really
cool community. It was like
nothing I'd ever seen before. Plus, she was making some real money and
she was actually helping people, but it was outside the conventional way.
Then there was me, still broke, trying to keep a broken furniture store alive.
Was Thea's coaching situation too good to be true?

You see, the lesson here is, if I had discouraged Thea from the health
program, or even tried talking her out of it, I could've cost us big time.
And again, my assumptions and saying no held up our process for a couple
of years.

To this day, our health coaching business has helped thousands of
people transform their health. How? Because of Thea's, and eventually my,
"yes." This has now become a full-time ministry to us.

THE HOUSE ON THE HILL

Now, I'd like to share with you another instance in the springtime of
2012. We were making more money than ever before. We were inches from
being out of debt. We were settling into a new, comfortable routine that we
were really enjoying—but that was the problem. We were getting comfortable again.

So, my wife had this idea to move across town on top of a hill called Bull Mountain. This would be something to stretch us (what I now call pattern disruption). But frankly, I was comfortable where we were. I made plenty of coarse comments opposing the move. But she started looking at houses. To which I said, in a snarky, pissy voice: "You can look if you want, but it's not going to happen."

The truth was, I knew my wife was onto something. Truth was, we had outgrown our then-current house. Truth was, I'd gotten comfortable. Truth was, the small groups and the weekly meetings, the health and hope nights we held in our home, were all getting old.

Thea found a house on the hill, and I agreed to go see it. As we're walking through it for the first time, though, I thought it was way too big, had too many rooms, and was wasteful. But what I was really justifying is that I didn't want to spend more money. This was pattern disruption, and I was scared to commit. To commit to a payment—and a house—of that size. I had always lived in fear of something bad happening.

Now, I had grown as a person, but I was still trying to live in an out-moded pattern. A pattern from years of debt, confusion, and depression.

My mindset had not caught up to my new reality of a growth mindset. And my friends, the next three months was proof of this.

Just one week later, we moved into that home with two big, empty bedrooms down-stairs—even though I had no idea what we'd do with this space. By the second week, it was time for the first health and hope night in our new home. We were further away from all of our friends than before, and way up on top of a hill. We sent out the same invites wondering if anyone would come, now that we lived so far away. Oh, did they ever! We doubled from twenty people to forty. There was no way they would have fit this many people in our old house.

Soon after that, this decision was even better. You see, those two empty bedrooms quickly became full. Thea's sister and brother-in-law were in a season of transition. So, now they needed a temporary place to stay. We had the space, and they moved in for a short time. We were happy to help them. And then, I got an unexpected call about my sister, Jen.

You see, she had been in and out of rehab for addiction and had a three-month-old baby. Her parole officer called me and said she was suicidal. But because of her baby, she couldn't get a bed anywhere in a facility that could help her. However, I had let her stay with us before and it hadn't worked out. So I had said she could never stay with us again. But this time I felt something in my spirit say this might be different. Because of her daughter, I said she could stay with us—but only for two weeks. And if she lied or broke any of our family rules, she was out.

Well, two weeks went by, and she was doing amazingly well. So I arranged with her parole officer for her to stay with us a little longer. The longer she stayed, the healthier she became, pretty soon her spirit was coming alive again. The next thing we knew, she was helping others, and finally a year later, this home had become a safe haven because it was far enough away from everything that our home on the hill did what no rehab center could do.

Eventually, she was able to care for her child and herself on her own. You see if you change the environment in which something grows, growth can happen. She was put in a healthy home with growing people. Today, she is a healthy, thriving, and vibrant mother and wife. In fact, she runs my conferences and other high-level entrepreneurship events with excellence.

Shortly after, another unfortunate family situation came up. My Mom and Dad were divorcing, and my Mom had nowhere to go. But guess what? We had another room. So, she also stayed with us for a little while until getting her things in order. She later moved to California. Now she's a thriving Grandma who lives near us in Arizona.

My friends, had I said no, I would've been closing off at least four other people's breakthroughs when I wanted to stay in Hillsboro, play small, and feel safe. Sometimes we need to look at the bigger picture, take our eyes off of just what we can see in the natural, and know that God wants to do MASSIVE things through us. But will we allow it? Or will we let our fears, excuses, and playing small and safe get in the way?

I can tell you right now, had we stayed in Hillsboro, I would be back in the furniture business, going through the weekly motions of life, wondering when my break would come. Oh, I had my break. And thankfully I took it. However, if you feel stuck, it's never too late. But we must stop saying NO.

STRUCTURE DETERMINES BEHAVIOR

Our underlying structure determines our behavior. If our behavior is inconsistent, it's because we lack structure and are operating more out of moods, or feelings. Instead we need to decide what we want most. We must pick one or two things and implement them TODAY and every day. They must be NON-NEGOTIABLE: "I do not go to sleep until they are complete!!!" Unplug the freaking TV and commit to YOURSELF and your DREAMS. Set the STRUCTURE right now and let it determine your behavior. Commit, don't deviate, and execute.

FIREWORKS FOR PHOENIX

Finally, we come to the last story of no I'd like to share with you. A few years ago, Thea and I went to a marriage retreat hosted by my friend and mentor Dave Blanchard. For the previous seven years, Thea had wanted to have another baby. But I didn't want to at all, and thought she would leave the whole emotional thing about having another baby behind us after we moved from Oregon to Arizona. However, she had not! And at the retreat, she brought it up again 😊.

We had an intense argument—and with her not letting it go for so many years—this topic got so intense I thought it may even be the thing that would take us down. She believed we were supposed to have another child. But I was happy with my two girls. We were going to start traveling the world, we weren't dealing with diapers, or strollers, or car seats anymore. No more crumbs covering the car! You know the happy place when kids graduate to this place 😀. For some reason I was so adamant about saying we were done, and I wasn't going to budge.

So, this particular week in October of 2015 we agreed to take one week off from talking about it so we could both think, pray, and spend some time apart—for me that included playing a lot of golf. That's where I can get my best praying in 😇. But after this week, we'd come back together Friday night and go on a date to talk about it. Frankly, I would have to give her an answer of yes to another baby, or no.

During the week, we were tired of being apart—but still really pissed at each other—so we went golfing together, but didn't talk the whole time! Now, I honestly prayed about it. But I came to Thursday, and I still thought there was no way I'd agree to having a third child.

Well, that day I was meeting with my personal trainer and very good friend, Casey, on a video chat and told him what was going on.

He listened to me for awhile. Then he asked me the question that would change my life to this day (and that my son Phoenix can thank him for some day). He asked: "Doug, has Thea ever been this adamant about something for so long and ever been wrong?"

I immediately said, "Holy crap" and thought to myself, *I'm having another baby.* My face went white as a ghost as my jaw probably hit the floor. I thought about all of the things she'd been right about . . . giving $12,000 instead of $1,200 . . . health coaching . . . moving into the house on the hill, I now realized, I needed to get ready to have another baby because this was meant to happen and why was I saying no to such a blessing.

Well it was because I had always had my life so planned according to my own goals and desires, often leaving no room for God's blessing and plan. Plus, I always trusted in God and Thea. Men, listen to your wives. They are usually right.

That Friday night, we went to the Hyatt Regency for our date to have the talk. I was dreading it, because I knew the answer, but I still couldn't make peace with it and coming out of my mouth only committed me. So we took a gondola ride, but the whole time I was struggling to tell her the decision I'd come to. My pride was making it *really* tough to admit I was wrong and she was right 😉.

Finally, I started to tell her as we walked over to the pool area and sat on a sun chair, even though it was dark out and we could only see stars. So I muscled up the courage and boldness to say, "Thea, this whole week, I thought there was no way I could have another baby." Honestly, it sounded like the preamble to a breakup speech! But then I explained what Casey said and how right he was. And I finished by saying, "Yes, we're having another baby."

I kid you not, the second I told her, fireworks lit up the sky as if I had planned it. Not sure how it all happened, but it was God's little wink to me of saying, "Doug well done, thanks for listening to my voice!" Soon it didn't take us long to get after it 😜 I think that night ☺.

A couple months later we were pregnant with my son, Phoenix. He's a purpose child. He is everything I could of ever wanted and I finally got my son. He looks at you with piercing eyes that can see through your soul. I know God has a HUGE PURPOSE for him and he was even purposely timed. I didn't realize our family was missing something, but now that he is here, we are complete with five. Plus, we didn't let the baby stage slow us down. We just made it work, traveling for much of 2018 visiting seventeen states and eighteen countries together.

START SAYING YES

I'm so happy I said yes in the five stories above. But honestly, I'm sure there are things in my past I've said no to that I might be paying the price for today. However, we all have the opportunity to start saying yes more often. It will shape our own future as well as the next generations'.

Let me close with this, men if your wife's on to a good thing, why are you fighting it? And women, if your husband is a dreamer and he needs to fly again, will you please get behind him and push him out of the nest? My friends, it's time we all start saying yes. It's time for YOU to start saying YES more often. There are much better days ahead when you just jump and go for it.

THE FASTEST WAY TO GET OUT OF A FUNK

On the days you are fighting yourself, fighting your emotions, experiencing self-pity, dealing with bad news, or just expressing a pissy attitude, here are three steps to help:

1. **Laughter:** Watch a funny movie or YouTube video, or call a friend to share a good laugh.
2. **Exercise:** Go to a one-hour coach-style class in which someone tells you and the group exactly what to do. Break a sweat and feel amazing. Sex with your spouse is also great for this 😊.
3. **Encouragement:** For one hour straight, send random messages of kindness to others with nothing expected in return. This is strictly based on adding VALUE to others. Add value to someone else by taking them to coffee, shooting a video, sending a voice message or giving them a call. Do anything you can to remove the focus from yourself. And if you do this step, it will quickly bring you out of your funk.

CHAPTER TEN

THE GOD CARD

For my faith-following friends, when you hear the commandment, not to take the Lord's name in vain, what does that mean to you? Seriously, think about it for a minute. What does that mean to you? Now, I'm willing to bet we're all thinking the same thing. It means avoiding using God's name as either a curse word or slang. And while I think that is part of it, it's not all of it.

Let me introduce you to something I've noticed in conversations, in coaching, in church circles, and with friends. It's on the rise and the folks don't even realize it. Here's what I have found the new use of God's name in vain is—and see if you think you're guilty of it (like I still am at times). I call it the "God Card." It means to throw God's name around as an excuse to say no! Because when this happens, we're actually taking God's name in vain.

Now, let's talk about a couple of the God Card's Greatest Hits I've personally heard in the last three months alone.

NEED TO PRAY ABOUT IT?

Have you ever heard someone reply to an opportunity by saying, "I need to pray about it"? I think people often use the God Card of prayer to delay obedience for what they know they should do. But instead of actually seeking God's direction, what they really did was shut down the opportunity for MASSIVE BREAKTHROUGH. I see more people miss HUGE opportunities when they say they need to pray about it.

For example, a while back Thea and I invited someone to a personal growth conference because we knew it would be an incredible breakthrough weekend for them, like it was for us the previous year. So we invited them to—of all things—a breakthrough conference with us.

We offered to cover their ticket, travel, and lodging costs as we knew this person was in a tough financial spot and knew this was a way to help. Thea and I decided years ago we won't just give "fish." We will teach people how to fish. But the first few lessons are on us ☺. So here we are inviting them to join us for an incredible weekend. Instead, we get a reply that said, "I will need to pray about it" ☺.

I replied, "Just to be clear, I'm paying for the whole thing." To myself I'm thinking what is there to pray about? This person has openly shared with me their life was in a rut, they were trying to figure out what is next, and money is tight.

But no . . . I then got a call the next day from this person. They said, "I don't think God wants me to go."

Okay, here's the tough part for me. I will never challenge someone on their prayer or relationship with God. However, I have a hard time believing God wouldn't want this person to experience a FREE conference and the people they could've been with.

Plus, it's interesting how I saw on Facebook that, while Thea and I were at the conference, God must have wanted them at a concert so they could relive the '80s ☺.

My friends, this is messed up. I don't know all the circumstances. But what saddens me is I don't know if she was supposed to go with us or not. Who am I to question? But I do know I will never ask again. I hope she figures it out. Talk about the broke journey of saying NO.

Again, think about this. I personally think where the Bible says, "Don't take the Lord your God's name in vain" IS not only about saying "Oh my

God" but also about NOT using GOD as an excuse for delayed obedience, or to manipulate or control a conversation by throwing out another God Card.

"GOD WANTS ME TO TELL YOU…"

Let me tell you about another serial God Card abuser. I recognize them as the people who walk up to me and say, "I feel like God wants to tell you that . . . ." And guess what? It's something that they don't agree with about my life. This is a slippery slope, my friends. You better be certain this is God, and not your own opinion. Play with fire and you're going to get burned 🔥 .

It's obvious to me when I'm talking to a career "God Card thrower" 😜, they are trained manipulators on how to shut down a conversation. And they truly miss incredible opportunities. These are often the people waiting on a handout—or an OBVIOUS sign from God—when they have passed up multiple billboards of opportunity. They stay waiting for the "perfect sign" that I'm not sure exists.

My friends, we must acknowledge and confront if this type of thinking and behavior has crept into our vocabulary, penetrating our minds and spirits. Has it infected our minds, families, and organizations? Has it prevented our growth? Has it kept us from the future we want, what the universe has for us, or even, dare I say, what God might have for us?

What if you just learned to start saying yes more often and open yourself up to an abundance mindset? More life, greater health, increased wealth, and generational blessings are waiting. Don't be more willing to put words in God's mouth than you are to take risks—and maybe even trust his path. You know, the one he may be showing us, even though it's not marked exactly with a dove, a church bulletin, or the voice from the sky like we want it to be!

My friends, pay attention, we humans LOVE the comfort of our routines—the ones that keep us safe: The comfort of Netflix. The comfort of our couches. The comfort of our bank accounts. The comfort of not getting phone calls from our creditors. The comfort of someone else's hard work handing me a blessing. The comfort of another weekend with nothing to do. The comfort of playing below the line. The comfort of blaming someone else. The comfort of saying, "He got lucky." (Yeah, lucky he's not lazy.) The comfort of depending on the state or financial assistance longer than we need to be.

I have a feeling that serial God Card throwers blur the lines of integrity. Because when we throw that card too much, we will find ourselves in more and more situations that put our character into question. We must ask ourselves, are we going to PRAY like everything depends on God? Meaning we literally expect him to do everything for us (and then when he doesn't, blame him for it)? Or, are we going to pray like it depends on God while taking ACTION like it depends on us 👊 ?!

Bottom line: by saying no via the "God Card," you may be robbing yourself, and your family of growth and breakthrough.

BELIEFS VS VALUES

Beliefs cause division; values bring unity. Spend more time finding things you share in common with others and less time trying to be right. Stop holding onto beliefs or opinions that cause division. This world needs you to step up and be a leader. It needs you to spend less time trying to convert people to think exactly how you do.

"PAY THE PRICE
TODAY SO
YOU CAN PAY
ANY PRICE
TOMORROW."

—————

—@THEREALDOUGWOOD
#CHURCHBOYTOMILLIONAIRE

CHAPTER ELEVEN

HEART OF THE HUSTLE

Recently, I spent two days at Disneyland with my family during the Christmas season 🏰 🎄. We had an incredible time together enjoying the VISION of what a great man—the quotable Walt Disney—had once dreamed.

"All our dreams can come true, if we have the courage to pursue them."
"The best way to get started is to quit talking and begin doing."
– Walt Disney

His words remind me that, for many years, I dreamed what it would be like to LIVE a LIFE where money or time didn't control me, my family, or my decisions, where I could literally LIVE a life on my terms, free of the control of others, a job, or terms set by a boss. And nine years ago, someone said something that has stuck with me: "Doug, PAY the price today so you can pay ANY price tomorrow."

Basically the way I heard it was, "DO THE FREAKING WORK." Stop talking about it, and get after it. Stop living normal, and get obsessed with creating the best life for you and your family. Those words play over and over in mind, which is also why we CHOOSE to LIVE an INTE-GRATED LIFE in which all parts become one. I talked about this earlier, but Thea and I used to have very siloed lives—you know, church, work, ministry, family time, friends time, and an attitude that wanted everything on the schedule, with nothing overlapping. I think some people call it work-life balance.

We just found the most fulfillment doing and pursuing what mattered most to us. As we operate in our unique abilities and help people thrive, we are most fulfilled. It truly doesn't feel like work. Except, people always ask me, "Are you working or are you playing?" The truth is, I'm always doing both. Don't get me wrong, I have boundaries. But why does everything always have to be separated? I have now realized this is why I use to be broke, not just in my mind but also in my bank account. Since most of the world works to live, I choose to LIVE to have purpose. And if you are on purpose, you will always be working but it wont feel like work.

AN OFFICE ON THE BEACH

Just a few years ago, Thea and I started traveling to Maui a few times per year to work and play and change the scenery; we love the water. You see, when you're not trading your time for money and you utilize current technology (more on this in Chapter 14), you realize you can work from your home, an office, a coffee shop, or, if you want to go to Maui, you can go to Maui and work from there ☺.

So there I am, laying on the beach in Wayalailai, still wet from the ocean after a good body surfing session and getting pummeled by the ocean waves. I grabbed my phone to check in with social media and how a couple of my clients were doing—and not because I had to, but because I honestly care about what they're doing and how their progress was coming along. As

I'm checking in, a guy walks by on the beach. He's old, wrinkly, and looks like he had spent most of his years working to live, and wearing some questionable swim shorts, I might add.

He blurts out, "What the hell are you doing on your phone? Look up, you're in Maui!"

I replied, "Excuse me?" as I thought he must have been talking to someone else.

He said, "You're in Maui, get off your phone."

I said, "I'm sorry sir, but this is my third time to Maui this year. I'm just working from here and enjoying a little bit of both."

He shook his head in agitation and I heard him under his breath saying, "Kids these days and their phones." He is right. Kids these days and their phones, if used properly, don't have to wait until they are 65 and shrively and miserable to go to Maui. However, he didn't know I'd spent the last six years working sixty or seventy hours per week grinding on my side hustle, creating a life of purpose, and working in my unique ability. And because of that, I'm going to offer you a vision of what's possible.

BLANK SPACE IS THE DEVIL'S PLAYGROUND

Blank space on your calendar is the Devil's playground for purpose drift, for getting yourself in trouble, and for feeling depressed. Understand this: You must get busy, and stay busy. Your time must be accounted for. Fill that calendar with everything that means anything to you. It must have your actions and goals built into it. So commit to your schedule and let your calendar own you.

DISNEYLAND DONE RIGHT

So back to Disneyland 🎅. My family and I were personally escorted through California Adventure and Disneyland VIP to the front of EVERY line. We even got to ride many of our favorites twice, all in about eight hours. Some of you will think this is ridiculous, and that's okay. But that tour guide cost us more than $4,000 over two days 🐻. You see, I don't like lines. Lines cost me time and a lot of negative energy is spent waiting

in lines. Plus it takes most people five days to do Disney and the reason is the lines, so why not eliminate the obstacle? Especially if you have paid the price and now you can pay any price to give yourself and your family an experience they will never forget.

Christmastime at Disneyland is amazing, but crowded. And while thousands stood elbow-to-elbow at Space Mountain waiting in line for two hours, we were walking through the exit in ten minutes or less. Let me tell you guys, it was awesome. And I make no apologies for it.

The night of the big parade, we showed up five minutes before it started and I sat back in the VIP section. We had reserved front row seats and I watched my girls, their friends, and cousin. I watched my son, Phoenix, giggle throughout the parade with the best seats on the route. And I had tears coming down my face, seriously. I was bawling uncontrollably with so much GRATITUDE thinking back to how hard it use to be, and also the daily sacrifice Thea and I made for the last eight years to create the life we have now. Part of the reason for the tears is I realized I had accomplished one of the many goals I set for myself a decade ago.

Then, looking out, I saw the crowds of kids and parents all around us. I could see pain in many of their eyes, even at Disneyland. So I looked at Thea and said, "We've got a HUGE job to do. These people don't know there is a better way. These people have lost the ability to DREAM. We need to lay out our path of exactly what we have done to get to where we are, so we can help FAMILIES HEAL, start THRIVING again, and CHANGE their family trees."

Here's why I said this. You see, just ten years before, I had brought my family to Disney on a prayer, credit cards, and saying no to everything my kids asked for. Because we truly couldn't afford it. You heard my story from 2008!

The reason I spent $4,000 on this VIP host is because I value my family's time and experience more than money. And besides, I've earned the right to spend some stupid money and spoil the heck out of my family once in a while and don't have to apologize for it!

(By the way, I encourage anyone to put this on your Live List. And what's a Live List you ask? Well, some people call it a bucket list. But when you're able to do it more than one time, it becomes a Live List! 👊)

I'm in such a state of gratitude as I want this experience for you and anyone else who desires it. And anyone else who will WORK to CREATE it. Because it takes a lot of work. Guys, seriously, it takes A LOT of work. It takes a lot of discipline. And beyond that, you have to be passionate. My friends, this is possible for you, too. Anything you have ever thought of or dreamed of, can and will happen. Remember, know what you want, know where you're at in relation to it, and it's the action in between that makes all the difference.

Because I'm going to be honest with you. During those two days at Disneyland, I saw a lot of fake smiles, parents saying, "No," and many people doing everything they could to live in fantasyland before going back to their real lives. But does fantasyland really have to be a fantasy? Or can it be "life land?" My friends, it can.

Regardless of what you do or what tools you have in your hands to impact this world, it will take operating on a different frequency than most people around you—yes, even the people closest to you. Remember, get around people who are GROWING and OPEN for more.

You will also need to take a hard look within yourself, saying, "OK, God (or your higher power) . . . I give . . . I cry uncle . . . Do you have something more for me that I've been closed off to?" Or maybe it will just take the understanding that creating what's next will take long days, early mornings, sleepless nights, new workout routines, starting massive conversations, being bold, living your LIFE out loud, or any of a hundred other things. The list could go on. But I will tell you what someone said to me: "PAY THE PRICE TODAY, SO YOU CAN PAY ANY PRICE TOMORROW!"

What many people don't understand is that paying the price starts right now.

- *Paying the price now starts with spending less time Netflix and chilling . . .*
- *Paying the price now starts by deleting some apps from your phone you know aren't serving you . . .*
- *Paying the price now starts by getting up thirty minutes earlier tomorrow and continuing this book or listening to a podcast . . .*
- *Paying the price now starts with getting in a workout or getting on a healthy nutrition plan . . .*
- *Paying the price now starts with holding up that phone in front of your face and pushing record to add value to other people's lives . . .*
- *Paying the price now starts by launching that ministry that's been on your heart . . .*
- *Paying the price now starts with writing that blog . . .*
- *Paying the price now starts with becoming a person of influence on social media . . .*
- *Paying the price now means starting massive conversations with people who are growing . . .*

Pay the price today (or for the next six months) so you can pay any price tomorrow (or for the next six years).

You see, as I'm working on this book right now, it's a gorgeous day in Scottsdale, where I live. It's early January, seventy degrees and sunny outside. I've been invited to play the most amazing golf course today, but I chose to say no. Most people are still on their holiday and dreading going back to work in a week, so they are getting as much as they can out of their time off as possible. I'm of course CHOOSING to be on my holiday and writing this book when I don't have to.

In fact, I've had it planned for a year to go to the Barrett Jackson car auction to buy a car that will be in town next week, I bought my tickets months ago to attend, and became an approved bidder—but then my heart tells me to get this book done. The truth is I've earned the right to go to

Barrett Jackson or play golf today. But I'm in the office working on this book. I'm committed to paying the price right now at a whole new level, so I can help thousands more people later. There will be more car auctions, there will be lots more days, or years, to go play golf. However, we must earn the right to do those things. Sometimes we must choose to say no to what we want now, and yes to what we really want later.

DOUGISM #19

PAY THE PRICE

It's interesting, a few years ago I had many people saying, "Doug, you need to relax, it doesn't seem like you have much balance. You seem so busy, like you are going to burn out." It's funny, because they are now the ones complaining on social media about their lives every day. They're missing their kids' events because of work. Also, some of these same people have asked me to borrow money. Go figure. Pay the price today so you can pay any price tomorrow.

I'M NOT IN THE MOOD

When I hear someone say the words, "I'm not in the mood," it's like nails on a chalkboard to me. And that's because of what my dad taught me as a teenager. I'll never forget years ago, there was a family friend's wedding that I did not want to go to. So, as a teenager, I thought I shouldn't have to ☺. You see, I was a young man and at the age of making my own choices. I remember saying to my dad just before walking out the door, "I'm not in the mood to go. I don't think I'm going to the wedding. I'd rather stay home and play video games."

I will never forget my dad looking me in the eyes and saying. "Doug, sometimes life isn't about YOU and always doing what YOU'RE in the mood for. IT'S ABOUT DOING WHAT'S RIGHT even when the mood has left you."

I went to the wedding that day and hated every minute of it. But even though it made no sense to me at the time, I knew it was the right thing to do. Today, I'm thankful my dad said that to me, because I have never forgotten it, and it has drastically shaped me to this day. When I have seen so many people living their life out of their mood, getting no results, I chose structure and doing what's right, or at least what I committed to. I have applied this principle in many areas, even into my adult life. Friends, I'm forty years old.

I'm not sure about you, but I'm not getting any younger. So, I'm going to encourage you with something right now. STOP living a LIFE that you're in the mood for. Quit whining about everything. It reminds me of the people who wear those stupid "I'm not in the mood to ADULT today" T-shirts. Yeah, what a great motto to live by. GROW UP and start being the CEO of your life. Do more of what challenges you. While I'm on it, remember that your kids are watching. They could sure watch you live more in structure and less out of emotion. Remember, you will never be in the mood to do some of the most important things. Things that will drastically impact you, grow you, and improve your future.

Growth, change, and success take getting uncomfortable. The feelings are never going to be perfect, and the stars may never be aligned correctly. But it's time to step up, kick some procrastination and bad moods in the FACE, and get some 💩 done.

Some of you reading this have some huge DREAMS that you have been praying for. Well it's time to apply some ACTION to those prayers and start flexing the hustle muscle. As my good friend, Bekah Eaton Tinter, says, "Don't feel your way into ACTION but ACT your way into feeling." And she couldn't be more right.

FLEX THE HUSTLE MUSCLE AND LET'S GET BUSY

This is gonna take WORK. Now, it's time to flex that hustle muscle 💪! If someone knows what day of the week it is, they aren't busy enough. I love when people say that Sunday is the day of rest or this day or that day. Re-read that part of the book. GOD took a day a rest after CREATING THE WORLD for six days. Not before!

Some people take Saturday and Sunday off even though they didn't do a thing Monday through Friday except scroll on social media on their boss's time, and then waited all week for their next cable reality show. The sad thing is, some of you are keeping up more with the Kardashians than you are your own bank account.

Your life has much more meaning and purpose than to just make it to the weekend, pay your bills, and start the whole mess over again. YOUR life is much too valuable to waste it week after week on things that don't matter. When did hard work, sacrifice, and busting your butt get replaced with, "Try your best," "Don't forget to take it easy," and "Don't work too hard now?"

I'm still chuckled by the people who were always thanking God for Friday—or dreading Monday or a certain day of the week. And they say it in a joking and sarcastic way. It seems that every Wednesday someone is wishing me a happy "hump" day. Really?! Happy hump day 🐫? What does that even mean?

Oh, I know the meaning. It's a meaning for all the people who have given up. Everyone who's waiting for another day, another week to pass by . . . To get the same check, from the same boss, so they can complain about it the same way, and then do the same thing all over again.

So, all you Humpdayers, stop humping and START THRIVING! Make today, and each day, count. It's time to get clarity on our purpose (we'll talk about that shortly), which will ignite our passion. Let's be FAITHFUL with what we've been given by CREATING the life God intended us to live! When you do this, I promise, you will not care (or even know) what day of the week it is.

When you are as passionate about creating your best life as you are about binge-watching Netflix, or your favorite hobby, you will quickly see the fruits of your work. I can honestly say the first four years of this process, I didn't turn on the TV unless it was the Super Bowl, or something major happening in sports. My golf ⛳ handicap went from 4.7 to well over a 9 (which if you don't know golf, that's a bad thing). And, I have successfully lost or been in last place in my fantasy football league every year.

It's all good, though. I had to take a few years to start WINNING at real life and less in my fantasy life. I had to buckle down, get serious, and not stay comfortable. I see a lot of people saying they want success badly, saying they'll pay the price for it. But they start taking their foot off the gas when they hit $5,000 to $20,000 in income per month. If you hustled hard enough to make $5,000 to $20,000 per month then $50,000 to $80,000 per month is not far away. Because clearly, you are on the right path in whatever hustle you have chosen. However, most people relax and start spending too soon. Because of this, they never get to taste the type of freedom of which they're capable.

Now let me be clear, I'm not saying sports and hobbies can't be done while building your next thing, because they can. But the point is, I was willing to give up what I liked and was comfortable with for something greater. I gave it up for financial security by not to settling and taking my foot off the gas pedal too soon.

Now, I can watch TV anytime I want (but actually don't watch too much). I just built my own backyard golf course, I still suck at fantasy football, and my handicap is on its way back down to a 4. I recently played Pebble Beach for three days in a row, and stayed in a condo overlooking the 18th hole. The point is, pay the price today, so you can pay any price tomorrow and actually stop shopping from the dollar menu.

BEAT THE ALARM CLOCK

What's your purpose? What's your dream? What's your meaning? Is your passion waking you up everyday without the alarm clock? If not, why not? Because it should, and if it's not, you probably need to figure out why real quick.

I know y'all are PRAYING—we all need God's strength. At least I do 🙏. But we better be hustling as hard as we're praying. PAY THE PRICE, flex that hustle muscle, and get busy. The thing is, this is gonna take WORK.

My friends, I'll tell you this—and I may put in on my gravestone—you are your greatest asset. Your kids and your family need their greatest asset operating at a higher frequency, at a greater level and faster pace. The bottom line is, they need you in the game moving much more quickly than you are today.

Get clear, get obsessed. Sometimes we gotta act our way into feeling, even if the mood is not there. Guys, this thing takes work, it takes hustle. I feel like I'm laying it out on the field for you right now. This is where people are missing it.

It takes more conversations. More phone calls. More videos. More authenticity. More prayer. More action. More quiet time. More conferences. More books. More podcasts. Less Netflix. Less video games. Less Facebook scrolling. Less blaming. Less complaining. Less sleeping in. Less apps. Less romance novels. Less magazines.

I will close with this. For some of you, it will take operating at this pace for three months. For others of you, three years. For me, it took seven! But I didn't quit. You're entitled to a day off here and there to recharge. But you've gotta get back in the game. You must make the daily commitment to be consistent to yourself, your family, your mission, your ministry, your finances, and the people depending upon you for BREAKTHROUGH.

WHAT WILL YOU GIVE UP?

People trade *time* for *money* every day. Some years back I traded in my low golf handicap to build a high bank account. Now I have both! What will you give up for two years to get what you want?

"DON'T GIVE FOR THE WRITE OFFS. GIVE WHEN IT'S RIGHT."

—@THEREALDOUGWOOD

CHAPTER TWELVE

THINK MONEY ISN'T IMPORTANT? THINK AGAIN

It's not your fault you're broke 🧍. But it will be your fault if you're still broke a year from now after reading this book. I'm sorry if somebody in your life told you that money is not that important. They really did you a disservice, and they're dead wrong. 🐝Money🐝 IS important!!! Now—I'm going to end this turmoil for you—just like somebody else did for me.

If you don't have much money, or always find yourself making decisions based on how much something costs, then you should change that. The world, your church, your family, and your kids could really benefit from you making more money. So many people think and say that MONEY is the root of all evil. But they kind of messed up that verse. The LOVE ❤ of money is the root of all evil.

I have found people love to butcher and paraphrase Scripture to help confirm their often broken belief cycles—the ones passed onto them through a father, a mother, a grandparent, a pastor, or anyone else they accepted counsel from. It's poverty teaching from a poor, broke mindset upbringing.

Please know, you are not a bad person for making MONEY a priority for YOU and your FAMILY. It MUST become a priority. Money is like a magnet. It will go to those who pay attention to it. Some of you don't like money. Some of you can't stand it and are sickened by it. How do I know this? Every time it's in your hands you get rid of it. You literally have it spent in your head or on paper before it even reaches your bank account 🏦.

Friday afternoon it's in your wallet, and it's gone by Friday night. But for the next two weeks we'll complain about our jobs, what we have to do, how tired we are, how long of a week it's been, all for money. So if it's not important, why do you spend forty to fifty hours per week chasing it?

MONEY REVEALS YOUR HEART

Let me be very clear. Making money and having a lot of it does not change you. It does not make you greedy. Money is neutral. It only carries the meaning we give it. It does not have a spirit. It just is.

You can do a lot of good things with money—and you know what? You can also do a lot of bad things with it. But you must understand, MONEY is neutral. It honestly doesn't care about you. It has no emotion, no mood. It does what you tell it to do.

In fact, if money is so bad, why are there four easy ways to give it every Sunday at most churches? You can text it, you can give on our website, our app, or you can drop it in the plate that passes by or on the way out.

I've seen people ruin their lives with just a little money. And I've personally seen people live the most generous lives without it as well. Having no money for most of my 20s and early 30s, I would still buy a stranger a coffee in line, constantly gave clothes away, gave food away, would pay my tithe most of the time (which I valued), and supported others where I could. We constantly opened our home for people to stay, gave away airline miles, and helped people even when we didn't have the means.

Now in my late 30s and early 40s, I still give and help people, but actually at a bigger level. As I mentioned before, I don't give for the write-offs, I give when it's right. At dinner parties, you'll constantly find me sneaking off to pick up the check. You will find me paying in full for my own missions trips. You will find me sending different families on full-expenses-paid vacations. You will find me sending money to families that I see on social media who are losing their homes to floods, hurricanes, and fires. You won't find me posting about all of this stuff.

You see, these are very small examples of the amounts Thea and I give. And I don't share this with you to boast. I'm strictly giving you perspective. Money just magnifies the heart. Whatever is inside will just get bigger. I make no apologies for making a BIGGER INCOME so I can now be a BIGGER BLESSING to my COMMUNITY. When there is a need I can be a first responder without having to check my bank account, or with my wife.

I have found money actually reveals the truth about people. My heart has just been magnified. And you know what? I've been able to make a bigger impact since I chose to make more of it instead of listening to people who said things like:

- "Doug, don't chase money!"
- "Be careful, money will go to your head!"
- "Hey, be aware of what success can do to you!"
- "Doug's book is all about him."
- "Doug's new book is him showing off."
- "Why would he name a book 'Church Boy To Millionaire'?"
- "Doug sold out."

And the list could go on . . . .

What's interesting is the people who have warned me about making too much money have never actually had any 😒. The part that's even sadder is that two of these people who warned me about money and made fun of my business have since approached me asking for A LOT of money! One of them the other day had his "mutual acquaintance" call me asking for a six-figure donation to save his church building from going under 🏛.

We've all heard other people say money won't make us happy. Well, I needed to test it to find out. And I can tell you this, it certainly didn't make me sad 😬🏆.

You see, no one living in abundance, who isn't jealous, or hasn't given up on their goals would ever say something so ridiculous. They understand what it can do for THEM, their FAMILY, and the KINGDOM impact it can make. However, I can say this: I spent most of my life without much money and I know what it's like to earn the value of a dollar—I respect it. You can do a lot more with money than you can without. Plus, you are not a burden to your family, kids, or church when it comes to asking for missions money, or whatever else you're doing.

See, money is a good thing. It helps in so many ways. It allows comfort, breakthrough, ease, love, abundance, peace, options, and more than anything, FREEDOM. I can LIVE on my terms and not someone else's. Again, that would be the real American Dream right?

Like I said, money won't make you happy, but I needed to find out for myself. The pastor of my church sure hasn't had any issues with it 😀. Also, try telling that to the orphanages we support in Guatemala and the Dominican Republic. Seems like it's making them happy 👏😬. And they are very thankful we got over our "issues" with making money.

What money will do is: send kids on missions trips, put jerseys on your kids' sports teams, provide private dance lessons, provide horseback riding lessons, increase your ability to tip 25 to even 100 percent if you want, pay off your debt, increase your quality of life, increase your tithe, GIVE with ease at the next campaign or fundraiser you are a part of, and, of course, weather unexpected emergencies.

The point is, making money is okay; you and your family deserve to be wealthy. Don't apologize for it. Success and money are beautiful words. Don't ever feel ashamed to talk about them or want more of them. When we were all raised, most of us were told to never talk about money or sex in public. Well maybe that's why our world is so jacked up with both of them. We were raised as if they are secret things, or don't talk about them . . . Shhhh . . . Well I think it's time we start talking about them. Because it seems as if both are pretty dang important if honored, respected, and talked about in healthy ways.

GO WHERE GOD CALLS YOU

Money has allowed me to live and be where GOD calls me to be, not where an INCOME calls me to be. I'll tell you this, money makes the holidays better. It's made possible all the missions trips I have financed myself, sending my family and many kids on. It helps provide better educations. And marriages sure improve when lack of money is not the focus of the fight, which it is for most.

It's time we PAY attention to money and where it is going. If income is controlling most of our decisions like:

- Where we eat
- Where we sleep
- Where we spend 40-50 hours per week
- What our vacations look like
- What our marriages look like
- What we wear
- What we drive
- And how much we can give to our churches or charities

... then don't you think it's time to start paying more attention to it? Or better yet, increasing it?

I've noticed more people around me seem to be broke, just getting by, struggling, and are always asking someone else for a blessing—or dare I say waiting on a blessing. If this is us, why don't we step up, take back power over our financial situation, and start creating a life of abundance. Because, ladies and gentlemen, this is one of the main places we must change our family trees.

Now, I know this is a little intense, but I'm bringing you up to speed on a quick read. I've spent the last seven years unlearning what I believed for the first thirty! I had to unlearn the negativity around money to now appreciate it. To accept the ABUNDANCE and the HEALTH around it, what it can do for others, and for my family.

MONEY AND OUR FAMILIES

My friends, hear my heart on this: no, money is not everything. But it must become VERY IMPORTANT, and we must put a priority on doing *good for others while* doing *well for ourselves.* I've observed a lot of friends and family that have left this earth either too early, or even at the right time, leaving their family with such a financial mess that they're not even able to give their loved one a proper burial because of lack of funds.

Recently, my friend Jordan told me a story about a funeral he attended. His friend passed away, but his family couldn't afford a casket, so they cremated his body. Sadly, they had little closure when his service was finished, because there was no grave to bury him in and no graveside to visit. Now, there's nothing wrong with cremation—as long as that's what you choose. But for this family, their lack of funds made the choice for them.

Not only did the person dying have no money, the family left behind had no money. So my friends, this is a generational beast that has been passed on. And frankly, I don't think it's right or necessary. When are we going to take personal responsibility for our financial situation and acknowledge the fact that money IS important and we can do a lot of amazing things with it. Even if we do nothing more than peacefully bury our loved ones without it being an unexpected financial setback.

So how about us? What is our status quo for how much money is important? Is it time to raise our standard? Hear my heart here, friends. This is important. No matter what city we live in, we must get our family incomes over six figures ASAP. We simply must. We each need it. Our kids need it. Our churches could use it! And we can make a bigger impact in a lot of people's lives starting with our own because of it.

INFINITE MONEY

Let's talk about one more piece of the puzzle before we close. For you to win, someone else does not have to lose. And for someone else to win, it does not mean you have to lose. See, a poverty mindset has you convinced there's only so much available and most people already got the cut. That role has been filled, so I missed out. That person beat me to starting that new business idea, so the opportunity is gone. Or the world around us says there are only eight slices of pie, and I need to get my slice before they're gone.

My friends, there is an infinite amount of money. There is a printing press printing off more money than you can ever dream of. And it's going to the people who will value and focus on it.

DOUGISM #21
THE BEST SKILL

—

I believe one of the best skills one can have is the ability to show someone how to become financially independent.

CHAPTER THIRTEEN

BECOME A TOTAL ASSET

Ten years ago, I would only attend a seminar or conference if my company paid for me to attend. Or if there was a church hosting a local conference. Of course, it had to be free!

Side note—red flag ⚑—run anytime something is FREE. Either no value will be given or a guilt trip is coming. Plus, it's usually rooted in a lack mindset which tells you everything you need to know.

Now, you have probably heard that most people have not read a book since high school. That was also me ✋. In 2010, I was making the same $60,000 to $80,000 a year I had made for ten years doing the same thing, volunteering the same amount of time, going to church the same amount, working the same amount of hours, carrying the same amount of debt, giving the same amount of tithe, and frankly, repeating the same year over and over. And I think most of us would call that the American Dream, right? Not that it was bad, but to be honest, I had burned out on life. I didn't see my family. I was depressed, and honestly, not that fun of a guy to be around. I think you know the story from previous chapters.

Finally, I decided to change things up, try something new, and invest in myself and my future. So I invested in myself (and again Thea was right) and spent $350 on a marriage, health, and breakthrough conference—and that didn't even include the flight ✈ or hotel room 🏨. And again, I fought her for every dime and penny. I told her why we had no business spending that kind of money when we had mountains of debt. I told her we could

figure all of this out on our own. After all, in my cynicism I said, "all these conferences just hype you up." I said it would be a complete waste of money.

Again, you guys must understand me, I was always a skeptic. I always had a mentality that people were out to get something from me, or take advantage of my sphere of influence. I'm not naive and I know there are some people out there like that. However, being a constant skeptic, shutting things down, and assuming the worst in others was not serving me well. But I didn't know how to change it.

So later, I'm on my way to the conference, in Dallas, Texas, with a pissy look on my face, saying, "Thea, this better be good. And we better get our money's worth. And I sure hope they have a sports bar."

Of course, the conference was amazing—and the content we learned is much of what I'm sharing with you in this book. I went home and applied it. You see my friends, what I was reluctant and saying no to was, again, the best path for me.

At great conferences they lay out simple ACTION plans with specific "how tos"— directions on what to do next—and in what order. They're not just hype, hopeium, and dream building. These are the places true awakening can take place in your heart, spirit, emotions, and living body. That weekend was a turning point in my life because of a hidden DREAM that resurfaced, and so I began to be repurposed.

I don't share that to brag, I just share that to challenge you to INVEST in yourself. Thea and I have invested thousands of dollars into ourselves every year since then through books, courses, and conferences. And frankly,

I think you should start too. We have become serial learners, and know that if we apply what we learn, we'll see fruit. But you have to understand, my friends, this was hard for me.

I went to church my entire life—and still do—and was raised to beware of false teachings. You see, I studied the Bible and memorized Scripture, but didn't read a book other than the Bible since high school. It baffles me to believe folks can read *People* Magazine, read romance novels, watch *Grey's Anatomy*, and have a serial addiction to Netflix, and yet these same people can tell me to be careful of what I read or learn outside of the church or the Bible 🏾. Go figure ☺.

However, when I started opening myself up to learning from everyone's life experiences, I learned there was much more fruit on wealth creation, emotional intelligence, social awareness, integration, servant leadership, entrepreneurship, and how to build a massive business or ministry in books I was warned away from.

Well, brother, I read them alongside my Bible anyway. I found that staying in one lane was stunting my growth. I was also warned against going to that conference with Thea. They asked, "Is it a Christian conference?" 😌, but here's the truth: Take away the worship and the altar call, but the Spirit was more relevant and present, and there was more hope, truth, and specific how-tos delivered in that conference than any Christian conference I'd been to. And by the way, over that weekend, I actually prayed alongside other men there about how we can up our impact.

When I was first introduced to marketplace ministry, I realized the church walls were expanding. I saw that the future of ministry, church, and business would look dramatically different. So I have learned, in whatever you do, look for the good—the fruit in every situation. Believe me, I also sat in conferences where something didn't align with my core values, so I left that speaker's session. This has also happened during many pastors', evangelists', and online sermons where I couldn't hear the same HYPE and HOPEIUM message again—I needed more.

My friends, I encourage you to eat the fish and spit out the bones in everything. If you are strong in your faith, you can apply the world's teachings through your faith filter. The thing is, I went from closed-minded and broke-minded, to open-minded and abundance-minded. What if I had been sitting under fear-based leadership? (And while we're on it, you shouldn't sit UNDER anyone, you should sit WITH someone.)

Now, you might say I'm a serial connoisseur of personal growth and becoming the best version of myself. But what I realized is that I'd spent thirty years sharpening my spirit. The truth was, my financial tank was empty. I had no tools and I had been taught nothing. Honestly, my emotional tank was empty as well. I'd been given few tools on how to win friends and influence people. I'd discovered few tools on authentic leadership and definitely not seen it modeled.

Frankly, I was raised to believe leaders don't talk about what's really going on, right 😏?

I hadn't been taught EMOTIONAL INTELLIGENCE. I'd wondered why I always had so much drama in my company. Why was everyone always blaming? Shouldn't I have been taught that at church? They cannot teach you everything my friends—and truthfully—it's not their responsibility either. It's your responsibility to find all the tools you need to operate at your highest level.

So, you will need to skill up, tool up, and constantly feed yourself in the four areas that probably make the biggest difference in your life: *financially, emotionally, spiritually, and physically.*

Podcasts and audiobooks must become a daily routine. Put them in the car. Your car should become a mobile university! Turn off the stupid radio or drama-filled station talking about daily gossip and find a course or marriage conference and get to it ASAP. Hang out at a bookstore, scroll through a personal development app, and start investing in yourself.

INVEST IN YOU!

A couple years ago I flew to Miami, Florida to attend Grant Cardone's 10X Growth Conference (because I choose to GROW). There were 1,850 people in the room learning from the best doers and entrepreneurs in the world. I was only three speakers in, and every one of them talked about ACTING on your PURPOSE, and adding VALUE to others as a non-negotiable in life.

So the average ticket to be there was $3,000 for the three-day conference—and that doesn't include flight or hotel in Miami Beach! The average income in that room was easily $250,000 per year.

I share this with you to show what the most successful people are doing. They are investing in themselves. They are reading more, listening more, and learning more. And they are ACTING on it, and starting somewhere, regardless of their income. They are tapping into free content online, or investing in the conference they know they need to be at, and not waiting for a sign or some magical moment for everything to change.

So, my friends, dial in your frequency—get around people who are growing. Get away from negative people who have given up on their dreams, ministries, lives, or businesses. Remember, if people around you aren't growing, run as fast as you can, because they will drag you down. People who desire GROWTH INVEST in themselves.

Remember this above all else: YOU are your biggest and best ASSET! You must invest in YOU.

STOP FIGHTING YOURSELF

———

STOP fighting the GREATNESS inside of YOU. The reason it seems so hard lately is because you keep fighting the TRUE you, the YOU that wants to RUN into your true purpose and desires! Maybe it's a phone call you need to make, an opportunity you need to take, a move you need to make, or a transfer you know is necessary. Fear is robbing you, your friends, your circle, and your family. It's time to step out of the boat, embrace the unchartered waters, and KICK FEAR IN THE FACE.

"**UNFOLLOW
PEOPLE WHO
ARE NARROW
MINDED, LIVE
BELOW THE LINE,
AND CONSTANTLY
FILL YOUR LIFE
WITH DRAMA.**"

—@THEREALDOUGWOOD
@CHURCHBOYTOMILLIONAIRE

CHAPTER FOURTEEN

HOW TO INCREASE YOUR INCOME

Recently, my buddy John and I spent some time golfing 🏌. We went to ministry school together, he was a grooms-man in my wedding, and is to this day one of my best friends who I spend time with. Well, I was fortunate enough to find my wife early. But John, not so lucky. Let's say over the eighteen years since I've been married,

he's been in and out of his share of relationships. And he hasn't found his Mrs. Right quite yet 😊.

Having said that, he has a great job as a successful project manager in Scottsdale. But on the golf course he shared that he would like to spend more time doing what he loves. So we went into the club house after the round, shared a cocktail 🥂, and I asked, "John, what do you love doing? What are you doing when you're most fulfilled."

After a few minutes, he replied, "Honestly, playing golf and giving relationship advice."

I replied, "That's incredible—I guess you have been in quite a few relationships and have some good advice as to what to do, and what *not* to do…"

We shared a laugh. He said, "Seriously Doug, it's what I love to do."

I said, "John, let's get you paid for it. And can you imagine the incredible wisdom and value you're going to give to others?"

Friends, I was encouraging John to live in his unique ability. And now I'm going to encourage you to do the same.

YOUR UNIQUE ABILITY

Now, a UNIQUE ABILITY is the essence of both what you love to do and are best at. It's your own set of natural talents. It's the passion that fuels you to contribute value to others. And when articulated, it describes the YOU that makes YOU who YOU are.

So, to operate in his unique ability, John would want to become a person of influence on social media. He would be giving away relationship quotes, memes, video advice, and all around incredible content to singles and dating couples. He's using hashtags, search optimization, and video to get in front of people all around the world. Very soon, John will be paid for these services. You see, if you give away enough value for free at the beginning, people see you as professional. And people pay professionals for their services.

My friends, you can become a person of INFLUENCE. You can add value from the stuff you already know, and very soon, be monetizing your unique ability, too.

How, you ask? By identifying problems and providing solutions. You see, this world has far more problems than solutions. And no, your unique solution has not been taken by somebody else!

1. *You're an encourager.*
2. *You're an incredible cook.*
3. *You're a great parent.*
4. *You understand health and fitness.*

5. *You have awesome communication skills.*
6. *You love to paint.*
7. *You create really cool Pinterest boards.*
8. *You have a designer's eye.*
9. *You're a great friend.*
10. *You love to write.*
11. *You're a fast typer.*
12. *You understand wine.*
13. *You understand technology.*
14. *You are a photographer.*
15. *You have great negotiation skills.*
16. *You're a brilliant strategist.*
17. *You understand graphic design and websites.*
18. *You have a unique gift or love for writing.*
19. *You are a person of influence.*
20. *You love to teach.*
21. *You love yard sales and bargain shopping.*
22. *You have an eye for fashion.*

Do you see, my friends, how this has already been created? You are good at what you love to do. There is a need for what you know. Technology 📱 and social media have now connected the dots between your UNIQUE ABILITY—or what you're good at—and are MONETIZING it. And more than anything, you can add so much value to people by helping them get clarity and solve their problems. That, my friend, is adding value to this world and making it a better place. And you know what, you deserve to be paid for it.

You see, unique abilities come in all shapes and sizes. For instance, have you heard of the comedian John Crist? Through viral videos 📹 he's become an internationally known comic of taking obvious funny things about his church in a very above-the-line way and making people laugh because everyone knows they're true. His videos have been viewed over one billion times! But do you know where he started out? Doing open mic nights at places like Chili's! But by sharing his unique ability through stand up comedy and sketches on social media, he's become one of the biggest names in comedy and is currently on a nationwide tour.

UNLIMITED EARNING POTENTIAL

I wish EVERYONE understood that if they just started adding value to people's lives by using their own unique ability and talent, their earning potential is unlimited.

TEN ACTIONS TO INCREASE INCOME

Here's the point: What John did is available to you, too. With his unique ability and taking massive action, he is traveling the world doing what he loves. So, I would like to share with you a path to do the same thing. Here are ten actions, if completely executed on, will help you monetize your unique ability—maybe even in the next twelve months.

One: Turn your smartphone into a mobile university.

Download books or podcasts (like "The REAL Doug Wood"!) to listen to and learn from. Delete the apps you know are time wasters. Get rid of the stupid games that help you procrastinate. Oh, and by the way, the radio station isn't helping you increase your income either. Turn your car into a mobile university.

Two: Unfollow or delete people living below the line.

Get rid of distracting people—the people who settle for average, who are narrow minded, who live below the line, who are constantly filling your life with drama. And maybe you even need to get them out of your life, and not just your newsfeed. This could be people on social media, people at church, or anywhere else in your life. If people are not encouraging, or have no growth goals, they are COSTING you and will drag you down. Don't spend another year figuring this out the hard way!

However, do ADD friends and FOLLOW people of influence who are doing what you want to be doing more of. Follow those who are successful and encourage you to become more. Fill your life and newsfeeds with uplifting, speakers of truth.

Three: Get your physical health in order.

Put in the effort. Find a structured health plan. And understand that simply saying, "I'm gonna do my best" doesn't cut it anymore. YOU are your best asset. Your kids and your family need you functioning at your best. Also, people don't follow those who they don't take seriously. And it's hard to take someone seriously when a very key area like physical health is so out of balance. It shows that self-discipline is clearly lacking. This is simply a DECISION to make yourself a priority!

Four: Become a person of influence who is worth following.

Start adding more VALUE and creating CONTENT on social media. "But Doug," you might think, "I don't have anything to say!" Oh, but YES you do! Everyone's an expert at something. Cooking, parenting, cleaning, the Bible, health, leadership, life hacks, shopping tips, and the list goes on. You must become a person of influence by utilizing current technology.

We all have value to give that we assume everyone knows. But they don't! Now stop being so stingy with your wisdom and share it. People are starved for value—and YOU have it. Be bold with it. Share it. And very soon, people will be paying you for your services.

Five: Only set GOALS, DREAMS, VISIONS with a deadline and ACTION plan attached.

Too many people (even leaders) out there are telling others to DREAM and have a VISION. The only thing missing are the simple steps and the consistent ACTION plan to accomplish the goals or dreams. I'll be honest with you, dreams without actions never happen.

Be honest with your currently reality; if it sucks then it sucks. But at least you can know where you are and can do something about it. Stop right now and set seven-day, thirty-day, ninety-day, and one-year goals. Start by completing the seven-day, build to the thirty-day, and make your way to accomplishing the one-year goal!

Six: Be more INTERESTED in other people.

Send a random text or message of kindness just letting someone know that they are on your mind, and they matter. Start authentic conversations without an agenda. People in sales or multi-level marketing, stop sending your buy-one-get-one free links! Nobody cares about what you have to sell until they know you actually care about them. And honestly, you don't even know that you can help them until you get to KNOW them. My encouragement is, serve people and meet them where they are at. Be interested in others.

Seven: Start a side business with your phone.

Ladies and gentlemen, we live in a day and age where social media is free. There will come a day when people say, "Remember when you could start a multi-million dollar business from your phone? When the rent on social media was free? When all you had to do was become a person of influence and add value and service to another?"

Start by giving away your unique ability or service for free, keep doing it, then do it some more. (Just don't get stuck giving it away for free forever!) The point is, your consistent delivery of value is when someone will be asking to buy your service. By then you'll create a product or service that people want. And start making more connections with people who are doing what you want to do!

Eight: Get on video.

Did you know that, according to Cisco, by 2022, 82 percent of all internet traffic will be video? It's time to get on VIDEO!!!! 🎥 Hold that phone up in front of you and push record. If they can LOOK into your eyes week after week and hear your heart for two to three minutes at a time . . . If they can see your passion for what you do, feel how YOU can encourage them, or how your services can help them, you will have PURE TRUST, a relationship, and very soon, a client for LIFE.

They will see you care about them, and not just the numbers or the money. Add VALUE to people at least a couple times a week. Become a dependable source daily, and not just on Saturdays or Sundays.

Shape your story and VISION by BEING ON camera. I know you are scared. We all are. I am every time I go live, but it does get easier. You will build confidence along the way, and it doesn't have to look perfect. People don't want your perfection, they want YOU and YOUR HEART.

I DARE YOU TO TEST ME. The moment you do this, you'll never trade that feeling, that shot of happiness when you help someone. And the best part is, your video will keep working for you, even while you're getting paid doing something else. It's time to get on video, my friends.

Nine: Become totally authentic.

Here's the truth. When most people turn on Facebook LIVE, they feel "obligated" to act or show up in a certain way. They feel constricted. Trust me, I went through this, too. Remember this, people want the real YOU, not your perfect, on-camera life.

When you live FREE you don't feel obligated to act or show up one way. You are just FREE to be who you are. And the truth is, people are actually more attracted to that. For the few that are not, stop thinking about them. They have made the decision to stay broke physically, mentally, spiritually, and financially. In fact, people who have made the decision to stay broke in these areas don't like seeing others get free! So forget about them and focus on being your authentic self.

Ten: Stop being so cheap and become OBSESSED.

You are worth more than you're probably charging, my friends. People want a professional, so stop apologizing for your price. In fact, raise your price. I know most of you reading this provide incredible services or products to everyone you come in contact with. But it's time. You may need to increase your value—but you must increase your price. The people you want to work with make buying decisions based on value, and your price often communicates your value. If you're too cheap, you're of no service to them. Stop being so cheap! The more you know the value you bring to others, the more confident you can be in what you charge.

It's also time to become OBSESSED. Unless you are crazy about your unique ability, why should others be? People follow passion and intensity. Remember, when we want something bad enough, we will become absolutely OBSESSED with it. When we're obsessed with what we want, ACTION to achieve it will follow. Distractions become noise and don't phase us. And believe me, RESULTS come after only a week or two of CONSISTENCY.

My friends, raise your COMMITMENT level, and you will quickly find the creativity to implement ACTIONS that will get you to your goal. However nothing starts without being absolutely OBSESSED WITH—and COMMITTED TO—what you want most.

Bonus: Promote yourself 😎.

Promote yourself, no one else is going to do it for you. Just look at the cover of this book 😏.

KICK FEAR IN THE FACE

My friends, you can GENERATE MASSIVE IMPACT by doing exactly what I've shared with you. You each have been given a unique ability, the thing that gives you joy and adds value to others. Maybe you're like my friend John, and give great relationship advice. Or maybe you're hilarious like John Crist. Whatever your unique ability, get completely obsessed with it. Kick some FEAR IN THE FACE. Pull that phone out, and press record.

BONUS RESOURCE

Use your UNIQUE ABILITY to INCREASE your INCOME!
Get your free bonus resource, the **10 Actions to Increase Your Income Checklist**, by visiting ChurchBoyToMillionaire.com

PROFIT ALWAYS FOLLOWS PURPOSE

If you are living on purpose and operating in your unique, God-given ability, you should never have to worry about profit. Profits will flow in abundance when you're living on purpose! Profit always follows purpose! Pay the price today, so your family doesn't have to pay the price later!

"**A** MISSIONAL
ENTREPRENEUR
KNOWS PROFIT
FOLLOWS
PURPOSE."

—@THEREALDOUGWOOD

#CHURCHBOYTOMILLIONAIRE

CHAPTER FIFTEEN

PROFIT WITH PURPOSE

Over the last eight years I've had the honor of helping so many people. I honestly feel like I've been in full-time ministry. When I started the coaching business to help people, I was having the time of my life. I was meeting with them weekly in coffee shops, talking on the phone, constantly texting, and even meeting up with groups. There was such an atmosphere of life and growth.

People were thriving and experiencing breakthrough. Honestly, think back to the best group of friends you have ever had, the ones who are the most encouraging and loving, and who make you feel so full—that has been my life for the last eight years.

Thea and I, after just six years of coaching, had never been so fulfilled in our entire lives. This was our side hustle, but it felt more like a ministry than a business. Yes we were paid, but honestly, we would've done it for free.

I remember talking on Facebook about my ministry, posting that it was good to be back in ministry. My friends, I've done more ministry in the previous six months than in my entire life before. It didn't look how I thought it would. It was connections, encouraging meetings, and praying for clients I was coaching. It was simply doing life together.

We have been doing exactly what I believe the church is moving to: modern-day marketplace ministry. Through this, I finally found my purpose.

"DON'T YOU GET PAID FOR IT?"

Please understand, both of my grandfathers (whom I love, respect, and adore) were Assemblies of God pastors and evangelists. I came from  a place where ministry happened within the four walls of a church building. So, marketplace ministry was weird to me. And, like I told you earlier, when I left school, I couldn't preach or play an instrument. So where did a guy like me go in ministry? Nowhere. I voluntarily entered the workforce.

So, here we are, years later, excited to share our newfound coaching ministry that was growing others and growing us, and helping so many other people transform their life, physical health, and well being. Plus, Thea and I were the happiest we had ever been and finally had clarity and fulfillment on what we were put on this earth to do. We were so excited to share what we were passionate about with the people closest to us—the ones who had our best interests in mind, or so we thought. So, we shared what was going on with a spiritual influencer in our lives. Let's call him "Tony."

I said to him, "Tony! Thea and I are loving our ministry of helping coach people. It's exploding! We have had so many opportunities to grow, coach, and help others. Plus, we've never had the opportunity to pray with, truly help, and encourage as many people as we have in the last six months!"

As I was talking, I noticed Tony's facial expression started to change. It was an interesting, confused, and perplexed look, like I was talking out of left field. Then he responded, "I don't understand."

I asked . . . "What do you mean?"

He said . . . "How are you doing ministry?"

I explained the situation over again.

He said . . . "But Doug, I'm confused. Don't you get paid for this?"

Now I was confused and frankly a little set back from being shut down so quickly. So I asked, "You're in the ministry and you get paid right?"

He stared back at me in shock and disbelief. The look on his face said, "*how dare you say that to me.*"

Then I thought to myself, WOW!!! He gets paid for standing on a platform and traveling around, speaking to churches, and accepting donations and love offerings. And I get paid for texting, phoning, video conferencing, getting into the trenches of people's day-to-day health and life. And I was doing it in the marketplace and coffee shops.

In the thought process of the great Jim Rohn, I said to myself "Isn't that interesting?" It was at that moment when I had already noticed that many of my pastor friends had declining church attendance. Church is going to start looking a lot different in the years to come. The most relevant will adapt and start to see things differently before it's too late.

I'll admit, I'd never been more confused by the comments from someone whom I had respected. It didn't rattle me though, because Thea and I knew we were on the frontline of becoming missional entrepreneurs.

So let me share with you what we learned: no longer do you have to choose between full-time ministry and a job!

People in MINISTRY can be SUCCESSFUL, make an INCREDIBLE INCOME, can drive any car they want with zero judgment, and can travel on their own dime without love offerings. People in ministry can be where God calls them to be and to speak, and not just where an income or the love offering calls them to be 👻!

PROFIT WITH PURPOSE

From time to time, Thea and I get asked to speak at different conferences. We are very selective of what events and churches we'll speak at; however, we respect every request. But when we become missional entrepreneurs living on purpose *with* profit, we can truly can go where we feel led. And we don't do it for the income! Thea and I wanted to be 100 percent in control of our time, income, and WHO and WHERE we are called to be, not where income, a job, or family call us to be.

Recently, Thea spoke at a conference but didn't ask for a fee. At the end of it, the hosts handed her a $2,500 check for her short, one-hour keynote. We didn't need, want, or go there for the money. We went because it fit with our purpose and we wanted to add value. Now, there is nothing wrong with making profit (in fact, I love profit 😋💰). But in that particular case we chose to re-invest the money into the conference.

See my friends, for ten years I was buried in a furniture store, learning, sharpening my skills, being stretched *without* profit, learning how to do sales meetings, and my unique ability was being SLOWLY mined, molded, cured, and shaped. These years were not by accident—nothing is. They shaped and grew me. God knew he had something bigger, I just wish I would've listened and quit three years sooner. But I needed that lesson. I was being prepared to make profit with purpose.

So what is profit with purpose?

My friends, if you are living on PURPOSE and operating in your UNIQUE God-given ability, you should never have to worry about profit. Profits will flow in ABUNDANCE to those LIVING on purpose! Profit always follows PURPOSE!

It saddens me how many people separate these two. They think if they're "on mission" (and not just a missions trip) in service to others, or in the ministry, they can't be financially profitable. There may be select times that's appropriate, but this mindset is no longer serving this generation.

If you're living in your PURPOSE and unique ability, fulfillment will be there, and profit will naturally flow. The reason we work jobs isn't *always* because they bring fulfillment, but because they bring us income—but we will talk about this soon. However, I do think any job or ministry should bring fulfillment.

MARKETPLACE MINISTRY

So you're saying, "Okay Doug, I'll give. I want to become more of a marketplace minister." Great! First then, please tell me your church has a coffee shop and you're not giving it away for free! Please raise your prices and use those funds for something at the church. I really hope your church has coffee mugs and t-shirts for sale, and you're using them to fund missions.

You want to get out in your community? Start a food truck. Wrap a truck and go sell coffee, ice cream, or food in your community. Create an atmosphere where you're taking church to them. I personally think your church should be creating jobs or generating profit to add value to the people in your community. This will further the work God's doing through your building, ministry, and people.

While we're on it, pastor, whether your church is thriving or contending for a miracle financially, please tell me you rent out your building—or at least some of its rooms—for people in the community who are doing good things—things that align with your core values.

Let's be honest, there are so many people in your community looking for places to gather and meet that they would rent and pay your church for services. Besides, I really don't think God gave us these big beautiful buildings, with big fancy sound systems, to sit empty five-and-a-half days per week, do you?

Is your conference room used all the time? If it's not, are you trying to rent it out to marketplace ministries or meet-up groups? If you are, then you are opening your doors so now people know what it looks like on the

A huge thank you to Mission Church in Gilbert, Arizona
and Desert Springs Bible in Phoenix, Arizona.

inside. And I will guarantee those people will start coming to your church. How do I know? I rent church buildings in Scottsdale, Arizona from the few who will allow us to. And guess what, we go there and give generously when we show up.

The point is, get creative, find a way to generate income with the resources God has given you.

JEN AND MARCUS JONES

My longtime friends from ministry school, Marcus and Jen Jones, had always kept in touch through social media. They were part of a thriving church. Marcus is an incredible communicator and pastor. And we would see them approximately once per year.

Then, over spring break in 2012 my family and I took a road trip all the way down the coast from Oregon to San Diego. We met them in a repurposing season. They knew they had a big job to do, and that they were called to San Diego. They were trying to plant a church in the heart of the city—and I'm not talking the beach part. See, this was a God-sized dream that would take God-sized profit. What they were doing wasn't going to be cheap.

They told us they were going to get jobs and plant a church. Jen told us she was going to be a barista and Marcus was going to get another job. They had some savings and were going all in. When we found out Jen was going to work at a coffee shop, we gave her a business idea that would allow her to work from home and use her unique ability. We even helped her with a plan to get started.

This pushed Jen out of her comfort zone. This was a complete pattern disruption for her plans. But she went all in, worked her tail off, and was able to create an income more than she would've made as a barista.

Very soon, the profits kept coming in, and she loved what she was doing. About that time, the church launched. You see, Marcus and Jen never had to get "jobs" because Jen started using her unique ability, and that came with profit to fund their bigger purpose. Soon, their church began to thrive. They rented a building and the church got to a place where they could pay Marcus a salary. But by this time, they didn't need it!

Their "side" ministry was now fueling their "main" ministry, and they chose to hire an associate pastor instead of paying Marcus. Then this lead to a children's pastor. To this day, I'm not sure if Marcus takes a salary but I do know they have a thriving church with a great staff and money doesn't control the decisions they make. As gifted communicators, they used the money Jen was making through her ministry. (Because when you're called to people do you really need boxes around it?)

Now they have a thriving ministry from home and a thriving church. They are now living on purpose with A LOT of profit.

How did they do this? Being the gifted communicators they are, they started recording two-week devotional series catered to men, women, couples, and every category you can imagine. They started giving away their talents and wisdom for free on social media. They cast a wide net expanding well past the San Diego city limits, reaching the entire world. Now, through their social strategy, they're attracting people all over San Diego to their church.

Their launch strategy for their devotional series continues to be successful. You see, their first and second ones were free. The third cost $10, then the fourth, $20 with a T-shirt. And then $40 for the fifth, and it came with even more value and swag for their audience, and profit for them!

Five years into this process, their church is growing. They just got their own building, and I know for a fact their online reach has become a huge net that's funneling, filling, feeding, and serving the people of San Diego.

Congratulations Jen and Marcus on planting and helping Center Church thrive in San Diego. (If you're there, go!) My friends, it is time that we live, build, and create profit with purpose.

PURPOSE DRIFT

You see, if the profits aren't coming in, the people aren't coming in. The sales aren't coming in. The volume's not coming in. Inventory is not turning over.

Instead, depression will start setting in. Blame-shifting and frustration will develop. Drama and unrest will enter your home, business, and ministry. Old addictions or secret-keeping will start to slip back into your day-to-day life.

If this is the case, I would ask, are you still on PURPOSE, or have you slipped into purpose drift?

My friends, I'll share with you, I've had two purpose drifts in the past nine years—even after being clear on my purpose. I was not that far off, but it doesn't take much. And my friends, you are probably not that far off either. It's important we stay focused on our purpose and maintain complete clarity on the impact we want to make on our family, friends, community, in our church, and all of this world.

Playing small does not serve the world. It's important we step up and live in our purpose—and please, create massive profit while you're at it so we can fulfill the purpose we were created for!

BE AWARE OF PURPOSE DRIFT

When you are in purpose drift, you feel forced to manufacture passion. When you are on purpose, you have intrinsic passion, the fire is lit. It gets you out of bed without the alarm, and you don't have time to scroll, blame, gossip, be jealous, drink, look at porn, or participate in any self-destruction that continues the internal tug of war.

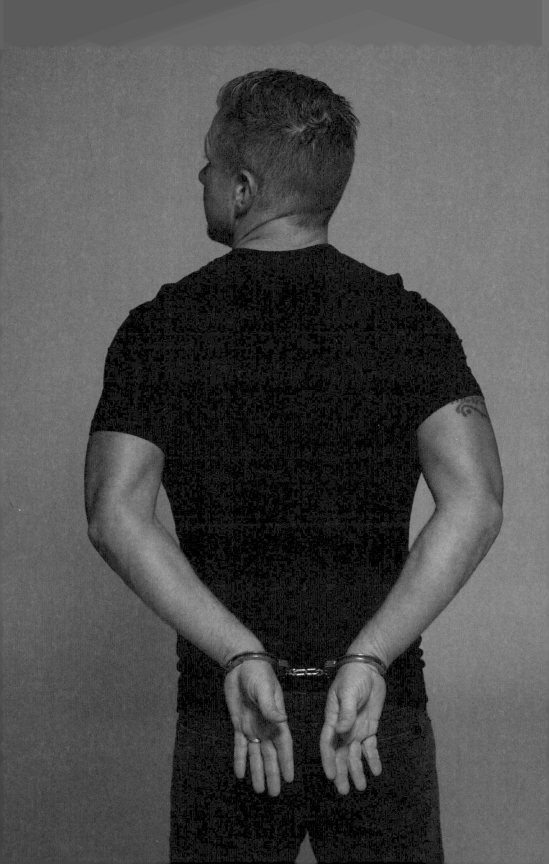

CHAPTER SIXTEEN

WHY OUR INCOME IS CONTROLLING EVERY DECISION WE MAKE

If you are like I was five years ago, you are probably living where you're at for one of three reasons. One, it's where you grew up. Two, your family or someone close to you talked you into moving (or staying) there. Or three, you have a job, business, ministry, or a means of income 🏕 that ties you there. And the reason why is probably in reverse order 😌.

At least it was for me.

You see, for the first ten years of our marriage, the reason we lived in Hillsboro, Oregon was because we lived where our family, friends, and business kept us. I literally could not move. And there was no out, even if we wanted it. Honestly, I was trapped.

That's why creating a life, income, purpose, and an integrated job and ministry that utilizes current technology 📱 is so important. You become able to work and play from your phone. You can let your content work for you, even when you are not working. I know I talked about it earlier, but in today's world, using today's technology, you must monetize your unique ability and income to add value to the world and not just your small town, and get current with trends and the speed of today.

See, for many of us, the jobs we have today are a means to pay bills. That's important, as we must keep them paid and we need to have as many jobs as it takes to provide for our family and do what's right. However, I see too many people spend too much time at a job they actually hate and doing nothing about it to focus and do something they love. Most people—including myself in the past—are missing what is actually most important to them.

We are giving our best years, best time, best energy, and our best focus to something that would quit on us tomorrow! The moment there's a bump in shareholder value, we're out. But they expect two weeks' notice from us 🤨.

How long are we going to build someone else's dreams while neglecting our own?

Five years ago, I decided I would NOT let any person, or any lack of income 💰, CONTROL my time or decisions any longer. I got so pissed at my current circumstances that I found a better way to CREATE and LIVE my LIFE versus REACTING to it. If you are not happy, if you want more time or money, then get pissed about it, make the shift, make the change, move (you are not a tree) and DO THE WORK it takes to create what you want most!

Last year, Thea and I chose to be in Las Vegas for a Friday through Saturday conference. The great but challenging thing was, our oldest daughter Amaya ended up getting the star role in the *Wizard of Oz* at her school. Curtains opened at 7 p.m. in Scottsdale, but the conference ended in Vegas at 5 p.m. What would we do?

In my former life, I would have to choose one or the other, and most likely I'd have to say, "I'm sorry honey, we have to miss your play." Or, I'd

have to quit on an income-producing action so I could be at what actually matters most.

This truly was my life in the furniture business—missing recitals, plays, and my kids' lives while working retail. I think I missed almost everything on weekends, because that's when the store needed to be open, and if the store was open I needed to be there.

Well, we live a new world now where we've created both time and money. With a little extra effort, we left the conference thirty minutes early, flying back to Phoenix. We saved an hour by leaving the car at the airport, bought roses on the way, and were in our seat by 6:45 pm that night enjoying the *Wizard of Oz*. Amaya was able to look for her parents in the audience, like most kids do, and see us both sitting there, present with phones and cameras in hand!

We took the family photos, laughed, and even cried. Then there we were, back on the airplane for our 9:30 p.m. flight back to Vegas to fulfill the commitment of our conference. Because we'd created time, income, and were living on purpose while doing both, we could be in two places nearly at once and the price of an extra airline ticket was pennies. Why? We were living life on our terms now. We had paid the price so now we can pay any price.

My friends, our whole lives we're given the choice to choose one thing or the other. Well that's the broke way in which we were brought up. I live in a world where I've created my life, and I want to have both. YOU too can have both—but you'll have to create it and it'll take work, sacrifice and clarity on what you want most.

DON'T SETTLE FOR COMFORT

Although this is a very positive example of living a life of freedom, there are also seasons to be prepared for. As I shared with you before, I've had two purpose drifts since rediscovering my purpose. Let me explain.

It was January of 2014, I'm living in the house on Bull Mountain in Tigard, Oregon that my wife was so smart to push me toward (remember, the one I said no to 😬). Our ministry and business were starting to thrive—which I'm just going to call "BUSINESSTRY," because if you're at this point, you should know business and ministry are the same to me.

I was making more money than I'd ever made in my life. Our ministry was actually helping more people than ever before. I had solid friends—many ABUNDANCE-MINDED. I'm going to a conference or two per year. Honestly, life was really good, and *really* easy. I was good at what I did. People loved and adored me. They would send me encouraging messages and tell me how great I was at conferences.

But in that season, I'd leave the high of those conferences, go back home to the rainy house on the hill, in just another dreary Oregon winter. I found myself slipping back into some old patterns and habits. Old eating habits crept back in. Sneaking down to Taco Bell after the family went to bed. Grabbing a couple candy bars and hiding the wrappers in the outside garbage can so my wife wouldn't see them.

I was starting fewer conversations with people and adding less value through social media than I had been before. Don't get me wrong, I could flip on that "I'm an awesome super-coach and I've got it all together" switch at a moment's notice. We're all trained to do a great job on the outside—but during purpose drift, we creep back into our holes.

The workouts had stopped. And I was going to matinee movies every day just passing the time until I picked up my girls from school. Thea was going through her own season of wanting another baby, that you'll remember I adamantly said no to 😖. Here was Doug, living a good and free life on his own terms, but slipping back into what was comfortable.

My income plateaued. I found myself unenthusiastic about going to church, not as excited to read my Bible of which I was once a connoisseur. I read fewer books. I listened to fewer podcasts. And what I really figured out was, I was in massive purpose drift.

See, at this point in my new life, most of all my problems were solved and my needs met. Many of my debts were paid. So, I backed off the intensity, and stopped taking the actions that got me to where I was.

This is a dangerous lesson I learned. Because if you know me at all, I will tell anybody you must set a new goal before you reach your current one. You must constantly move the goal further and further ahead, always asking yourself, "What's next?"

My friends, I've learned this the hard way. Please trust me in this. It baffles me that I backed off the closer and closer I got to reaching my goals. This has always been related to my debt payoff, my weight loss, or any other goal I've set for myself. Why? Because I'd always met and lived a life of just-enough syndrome.

See my friends, that's the frickin problem! I'm absolutely sickened by how we do this to ourselves. Why have we chosen to live up to a certain expectation that *someone else* (or we ourselves) have set and call it good enough?! I reached another pivotal point in my life where I could no longer accept good enough.

Too many people around us are telling us we're good enough, so chill out. People told me, "You have an amazing life Doug—relax a little bit. Look at what you've built over the last few years. Do you have to work at this pace forever?" But whenever I did back off, they stopped saying anything. The messages quit coming. And I'm left lonely and frustrated, and frankly, I was unfulfilled when I was going at the average speed.

I've realized I hate the person I am when I back off to Netflix and chill—don't get me wrong, the chilling's cool 😜. But every time I get back into the nightly soap opera of Fox News and CNN, downloading my TMZ app again, going to an obsessive amount of movies, or simply biding time until my passion would reignite and make me happy.

This is exactly what was happening.

NO REPLACEMENT FOR OBSESSION

So there I was in Tigard, and for the first time I decided to see an acupuncturist. (If you've never tried it, it's awesome.) I was trying oils, trying to work out with zero motivation, my prayer was off, and all around, I was on autopilot. However, I quickly learned there is no acupuncture cure or essential oil to replace this: "Doug, get clarity and get obsessed about what's next."

In fact, if someone could create that oil or acupuncture needle, they'd probably be a millionaire! But lemme tell ya', no one can create it but you!

Soon after, we were going to a friend's wedding in California. Thea and I were on an airplane and opened up the magazine in front of us, looking at at all the places we have to travel that summer.

You see, three or four weeks later our lease was up on that house on Bull Mountain, and we were wondering what should be next because even some of our friendships were no longer feeling the same. The truth was, we knew we needed a pattern disruption. For us at that point, it would've been a new gym, new church, or maybe even moving to a different side of town again.

However, I will say this, while those can be great pattern disruptions, we knew we needed to totally disrupt status quo if we were going to go to another level.

Sure, we had some discontent over having another baby. She knew I was struggling again in my HEALTH and NUTRITION. But we had come together on common goals without picking apart each other's weaknesses. We were called to fulfill God's plans on our lives. We realized that income with lack of goals made us too comfortable—and unfulfilled.

After the wedding, and many conversations, we're on a plane again headed home. We're landing back at Portland International Airport ✈ after enjoying the sunny wine country of Temecula. And the pilot says in that nasally pilot voice, "We'd like to welcome you to Portland. It's a nice, rainy forty-five degrees with a thirty miles-per-hour crosswind . . . ."

You know what I'm talking about ☺.

Thea and I looked at each other and said, "You wanna go on an adventure?" The lease was coming up, the school was coming up, and it was time to make decisions. We couldn't continue any longer the way it was. Life was good, but we weren't busy. We were just going through the motions of living with a higher purpose and higher income. We were giving at a higher rate and supporting missions more than ever before. But still, it was time for a pattern disruption.

We made a call. And within three weeks we were moving everything we owned from our house on the hill into a storage unit. We lived out of our car in hotel rooms, and stayed with friends for the entire summer on

a road trip throughout the Western United States, bouncing from California to Texas to Nevada and then to Arizona 🌵.

You know what? That was the most fulfilling and bonding summer in our family's life. We laughed, giggled, and stayed in some very interesting hotels. We cried, we were lonely, we missed our friends, we missed normal, and even missed our family. We were also prepared for the hell we were about to catch—but we knew we couldn't go back.

We landed in Scottsdale, Arizona and made a commitment not to move anywhere for people. And for the first time in our lives, we lived where God called us to live, not income. We didn't know why, but we fully committed. Everything was different—new doctors, new driver's licenses, and new surprises. But we'd never had more clarity and pure joy than ever before.

TIME TO EXPAND

I'll close with this. I didn't know where that twenty-year-old, passionate, I-want-to-change-the-world, crush it, do great things, be a pro-athlete, be a singer, starry eyed church boy had gone.

It is a scary place to be when something that was once a calling, purpose, or passion has descended into old, boring, status quo, just enough, let's get by, or dare I say, just a job. The same old grind, same old Sunday, same old emails, another month of missed quotas, mindless nights and days scrolling on social media, unmet expectations, and just trying to make the mortgage. Or maybe like me, the mortgage isn't the issue and it's truly about fulfillment and joy for you. I have a feeling more of you are at this place than not. Trust me, I know what it feels like when the fire turned to a wisp of smoke.

I have a feeling you are creating something absolutely stunning, something you're so much closer to than you even realize. But we must act—and it could take a pattern disruption. It could be as small as moving across town. Or it could be as big as traveling the country in your car for a summer!

My challenge for you is this: it's time to expand, grow, get creative, repurpose, and create a NEW YOU and a NEW SEASON. Your SPIRIT, FULFILLMENT, and living in your UNIQUE ABILITY depends on you letting go and kicking some fear in the face!

POVERTY WAGES

———

If you are "on staff" at a business or church that is paying you (almost) poverty wages but still TELLS you where you can, or cannot, have a side hustle, you are a part of a broken system. I say this in pure love, but it won't be long until you are left broken.

I see too many AMAZING people give their best years to being chewed up, underpaid, and left with no opportunity to better themselves or their family. Yes, it's about SERVING, but how can you serve at your best when you and your family are BROKE? When you practically have golden handcuffs on?!

It's OK to take care of YOU and your FAMILY! Serve YOUR DREAM and your family for a change this season.

ISRAEL

ICELAND

PARIS

GERMANY

LONDON

EUROPE

SINGAPORE

DOMINICAN REPUBLIC

"A SCARY PLACE
TO BE IS WHEN
SOMETHING
THAT WAS ONCE
A CALLING
OR PASSION
BECOMES JUST
A JOB."

—@THEREALDOUGWOOD
#CHURCHBOYTOMILLIONAIRE

CHAPTER SEVENTEEN

NOT PAYING BACK IS A B!+¢# 😜

Part of cultivating an abundance mindset is understanding how important the promises we have made to other people and to God truly are—promises we have possibly broken or even forgotten about.

I will never forget a pledge 💰 Thea and I made years ago to a church in Portland for their new building fund. We were not guilted into pledging with a promise of reciprocal blessing, however, it was a challenging financial season. But we still committed a monthly pledge of $200 as we knew that would stretch our faith, ourselves, and contribute toward this mission we were a part of.

Just like always, things were tight financially (though not as tight as other times). But after we'd paid about half our pledge, we moved to the other side of town and began attending a different church. We justified that, because we left, we didn't need to keep paying. So we quit. But who's building was that? The church's or God's? It was God's. So, did we make a pledge to the church or to God?

At the time I didn't think much of it. But years later, I couldn't shake that unpaid commitment. There was something in me that didn't feel right about it, but I ignored it for the next few years. Though it kept percolating as our finances continued a downward slide. And this helped us further justify that we couldn't pay, because we needed the money.

I'm not saying we were being punished. I'm simply saying that not paying what we owe comes with a steep price tag. Sometimes it's the price of lost sleep. Sometimes it's the price of future blessing. Sometimes it's the price of conscience—not doing what's right and knowing it. Sometimes it's the price of friendship.

WHERE HEALTHY FINANCES COME FROM

For the next few years we couldn't shake this feeling of debt. We realized we made a commitment, but it was more about us fulfilling the commitment to ourselves and God, rather than just to a church building 🏛. Now, you need to understand, at this point we were still in massive debt and liquidating my first furniture store. Things weren't good financially.

However, we knew we had to start paying, even a little. We scratched about twelve checks over the next year. We had to get that debt off of our conscience. You see, healthy finances start by not cheating ourselves and making good on our promises to our Creator and others along the way.

I truly believe this was us breaking the generational financial strains that had plagued our family. Paying back and making good on a promise is one of the key ingredients in the abundance mindset.

DEBTS AND OWING PEOPLE MONEY

I know you're dying to keep reading this chapter 😜. But I think it's an incredibly important point, because it's one of the reasons my family and I live in financial abundance to this day. Remember when I shared earlier that abundance is a mindset?

Just to be clear, debt is rarely a good idea. But often it's all we know or the only way forward we see. However, as I personally know, desperate times call for desperate measures and conversations.

I will never forget the dark season of 2007, where the book began, where I finally went to my dad, asking to borrow $40,000 to keep inventory flowing, make payroll, and buy enough time to save my company. It was the most humbling and humiliating conversation I've ever had.

If for some reason you are comfortable with borrowing, asking for money, and owing debts, then it's time. YOU MUST confront that beast head on! This should not be normal or comfortable. It should make your skin crawl. Desperate times do call for desperate measures. But for many, this is not desperation, it's a habit! And in order for things to change, this mindset must change.

Once I took the walk of shame after borrowing money from family, I told myself I would not be responsible for messing with my parents' retirement. It's funny how we'll actually work harder for someone else than we will for ourselves. I don't know how many hours I worked in those days, but I think it was close to 80 hours per week.

Even though I owed a lot of creditors money, I made sure my dad was paid back first. Why?—honor, relationship, and what little bit of self-respect I had left. By the grace of God, hard work, and flexing the hustle muscle, I eventually paid everyone back—but Dad got paid FIRST.

Also, while I was in debt to him I didn't go out to eat much, or spend even $10 extra, until he was paid. Some weeks I remember paying him just $25, or whatever I could. You have to understand, this was humiliating. I knew he didn't need the money—actually, that's dead wrong of me to assume! That's none of my business. What *was* my business was me making weekly payments to him so he knew I hadn't forgotten and I kept reminding myself.

It was principle. You see, I wasn't going to ruin a relationship, have any awkward family hugs, or feel shame around him because I wasn't taking care of my money… which meant I needed his.

Don't worry, he's been paid back in full, as I took him to the Master's a couple years ago.

Speaking of honoring relationships and money, I can't even tell you how many "friends"—many of them "church friends"—back in the day would come into my furniture stores hinting, or just straight up asking, for a discount. Or they wanted to buy at my cost. Even worse was when I got that weird look insinuating that I should be "hooking them up" (so awkward). Crazy, I know, right?!

I have an idea for this type of person: instead of asking for a discount, why don't you hook them up with support and encouragement for putting their lives and families on the line, for doing what they do and chasing their dreams.

Now, I'm not in the small business industry anymore, and don't have to deal with price negotiations, but can I encourage you all to support your friends and family who are? They need your support. You should even pay full price or more just to do business with a brother who is doing right, living right, working hard, and probably giving a portion of the proceeds to a good cause, to God, or to sending some young world changer on a missions trip.

Pay full price, walk out with your head held high in an ABUNDANCE MINDSET. Go bless somebody!

CHEATING OURSELVES

Here's my encouragement to you reading this: If you do borrow money, or are ever in the place you need to borrow, make borrowing from family or friends your last resort. And if you do, pay them back first—yes, even if it's only $1 a week. It's principle, and lets them know you haven't forgotten. Even if you think they don't need the money. (Remember, that's not the point, not for you to decide, and not an okay justification.) Plus, self-honor, self-respect, and your effort show more than the actual money most of the time.

On the other side, don't loan money if you ever expect to see it again. If you are not in a healthy financial position to do so, it can ruin a relationship, and you are probably harming your own family by putting yourself at risk. Plus, Thanksgiving dinner just doesn't taste the same when you are in debt to someone you're sitting across the table from.

If someone has borrowed and has not paid you back and it's really bothering you, then I encourage you to let it go and count your losses. That's on them and their integrity. We are not the judge. They will pay the price because no one ever gets a hall pass.

What I have learned from loaning money is I have often enabled a negative situation that is perpetual in someone's life, which is why we should be discerning when loaning (or gifting) money.

To sum this up, if you do owe someone money, regardless of if it was ten years ago, have the self-respect to start paying it back—even if it's $10 a month. ABUNDANCE starts in the heart and making good on past promises. I invite you to do something Thea and I did that was a major part of breaking the financial beast that always hovered over us.

Who might you owe money to that you know, or maybe forgot about? Take inventory of these people and amounts. The reason I listed mine out for you is it's time that we take personal responsibility and we play above-the-line in this arena. This is a key ingredient in creating ABUNDANCE which leads to HEALTHY RELATIONSHIPS and FINANCES. Healthy finances start by not cheating the system or anyone else, because this just cheats ourselves of learning and living a life of abundance and freedom.

BONUS RESOURCE

Pay INDIVIDUALS before institutions! Get your free bonus resource, the **Personal Debt Inventory Worksheet**, by visiting ChurchBoyToMillionaire.com

LET IT GO

———

The bigger person always makes the first move; especially when staying still is causing unhealthy internal dialogue. Yes, you may have been hurt. You may also be able to justify that something bad that happened is someone else's fault, or that they need to come to you to make it right. However, I encourage you to forgive and move on, even if it's just in your own mind and spirit. Holding onto unforgiveness causes too much pain and consumes too much energy because of the amount of energy you spend thinking (and talking) about that person or situation. Let it go.

CHAPTER EIGHTEEN

WHY MY TEENAGER CAN RAISE MORE MONEY THAN YOU

A side effect of making abundant MONEY—or becoming a MIL-LIONAIRE—is you get more puppy-dog eyes from your friends and family. You'll find the assumption that you're supposed to pick up the bill—or cover more than your share for a group expense. Side note: I would've picked up more than my share anyway, until people started making assumptions and comments that just because I make a lot of money, they shouldn't have to sacrifice and I should. (Oh, you want to talk about sacrifice? You mean my early mornings and late nights while you've been Netflix and chilling?)

People ask me for money all the time, or to support them to launch their company, passion, mission, or church. They ask for monthly support, weekly support, and the list of support could go on. I've often given one of two options to people who ask. First, I offer a couple of coaching sessions to teach them to do exactly what I have done and become financially independent—much I've shared with you here in this book. The second option is for me to simply consider supporting them. But what I was really feeling out is did they want to learn and grow, or did they just want my money?

Shockingly, most wanted my money and monthly support if "God laid it on my heart." However, often these same people had told me that money is not that important, which is funny because it seems a habit that they never have it but always ask for it. To be honest, giving someone money is actually a much easier thing to do. Money is replaceable, my revenue streams are recurring. I've made it a lifestyle because I know the impact it can make on the world and the FREEDOM it gives my family to move about the country 😊. However my time—that I offer through coaching— is something I can never get back. And it's really invaluable if applied.

You see, I actually protect my time more than money. Ask anyone who knows me well. We bought our home, Breakthrough Acres, in Scottsdale, Arizona 🌵 in the summer of 2016. Many of you have been there. These are sacred grounds to us because we created an environment of peace and restoration where time just slows down. That's how important it is.

But the real problem is the people asking for money actually need my time more than they do the money! Oh, what you could learn from people who have done what you want to do! It would be far more valuable than money! They just don't know it. I find this a vicious cycle—it certainly *was* in my life.

Do you remember my story about asking Phil Mickelson for money? If Phil would ever get my letter today, I would ask for an hour of his time. I don't need his money and wouldn't take a dime. But Phil's time is so valuable, especially when looking at the charitable impact he's had on this world. I could learn so much from him.

ASKING FOR "SUPPORT"

I want to be very clear. Asking for support is not a bad thing. It depends on the who, where, when, why, and the heartbeat behind the ask. Honestly, it depends on the relationship you have with the person you are asking. I had no business sending Phil Mickelson that letter ten years ago asking for a handout. First of all, I don't know Phil. Secondly, I'd never given him any encouragement or value. Third, I did it by email 😬. I had zero relational equity to ask Phil for a handout.

So, in the last few years I have received many emails and messages asking for support to go on missions trips. The only thing that baffles me about it is the people I'm getting letters from have not been in relationship with me in any way. They don't comment on my social media posts very often. I don't even get a Christmas letter 😕. I have some of these people as contacts in my phone—but I don't even get a text a year, not even a "Happy Birthday."

However, it chuckles me when I only hear from them when they need *prayer* to go on a missions trip. But in the fine print they also mention it would be wonderful to have money, if "you feel so led" 😌. It still baffles me, the order that they ask. I know what they want and so do you. But I think we code the letter in vain, throwing a major God Card.

Now, I think missions are great. I know first-hand what an impact they have on the people being reached in foreign countries, as well as on the people going on the trips. Personally, I've been greatly impacted while on missions trips my entire life, which is why I'll continue to go on many more. I love missions.

However, there is something that my parents taught me to do when I was in junior high that—while I hated at the time—I now thank them for. It has shaped me into who I am today and influenced much of my ability to write this book. I believe this issue is where the abundance mindset can begin for people.

As a kid, if I wanted to go on a missions trip and asked for support, I had to pick up the phone, call adults and ask for money. I had to let them know I was going to send a handwritten personal letter (not copy and paste) explaining a little about my trip, and ask if they would consider financially supporting me after they received my letter. And I'll be honest with you, I didn't say much about prayer because I knew why I was calling—and so did they. I also made it very easy for them, including a self-addressed stamped envelope.

It was a hard and humbling thing at the time, but it was something my parents wouldn't do for me. They wouldn't even gather the addresses, or in today's world, send the Facebook message, for me. If I wanted to go, I'd better get to work mowing lawns, have a garage sale, host a car wash, or sell lemonade. And first, they always told me they weren't giving me any of the money (at least that's what they said). But guess what? If I wanted to ask for something I had better be invested in it. Then, between the car washes, mowing lawns, and asking for support, I raised the money.

DOUGISM #28

DO WHAT'S RIGHT

———

ABUNDANCE and financial breakthrough
start with making RIGHT on past debts.

These days with technology and these phones 📱, it's ten times easier to make money if parents would help these kids get creative and work for it. However, I'm seeing many copy-and-paste emails from parents asking for their kids. Or even just getting direct links to GoFundMe accounts without any explanation or dialogue, without any context of the WHY behind the trip. That's called cop-out and spam.

Also, let me just say, if we haven't talked or communicated in a over a year, but I'm sent a random GoFundMe link without communication, in a copy-and-paste letter, and lacking any personal touch, that's just horrible communication and bad social awareness skills! At least wine 🍷 and dine me 🍽️!

In today's social-media-driven world, I would encourage kids to use video to bring people into both their passion and reason why for their mission. Seriously, who can say no to a heartfelt video with a junior higher or teeneager sharing their passion for going on a missions trip?

Also, there's nothing wrong with sharing a GoFundMe page to make it easy for people to give. Just do them in the right order and don't be spammy. Engage and pull people into what you are doing with video and you will raise your money, as long as you are working hard on your own. Make sure people know what and how else you are raising money. People need to see your hustle. They want to know you are doing more than your part, and not just asking for handouts.

THE ABUNDANCE ASK

On a side note, just to set the record straight, Thea and I believe that young people, up through college age, could use some help going on their first or second missions trip. We also believe there is an ABUNDANT way you should ask for support.

As I've grown older and cultivated an abundance mindset, I've realized how often adults put their family at risk going on missions trips. They may be leaving town for too long or too often, with the intent to serve, but really, are doing a disservice to their own family. How? By putting their entire financial livelihood at risk! Ministry starts in the home. And I have a hard time believing people are #called to go on a missions trip when they've yet to fulfill their calling to their family—and yes, I am talking about finances 💰. This is where you must start creating time and financial margin in your life.

DEAR MR. OR MRS. ADULT

Dear Mr. or Mrs. Adult, why are you leaving any unfinished business back home? You have unpaid bills, debts, are stressed out, and frankly, are one to two paychecks away from living on the streets. I know this is blunt and bold, but I am @TheRealDougWood, and I'm going to keep it real for a few more minutes 🔊.

Mr. or Mrs. Adult, is this really your best season to go on this trip? Please hear my heart. Missions are important, but what is most important to your mission? What about your mision back home with your family, and your responsibility? Ask yourself, is this missions trip really for me, or is it genuinely for the kids in Africa? Sadly, it's become more about the person going and less about the mission itself.

Now before you throw this book in the fire, I say this for one reason: *this is what "paying the price today, so you can pay any price tomorrow" is all about.*

It's paramount that you put the oxygen mask on *yourself*—*your family*, *your finances*, and *unfinished business*—before assisting the passengers next to you. You may not agree with me here. And you don't have to. There are plenty of other ways you can get to Africa if it's on your heart.

There will be another trip—but maybe you're going to spend the next twelve months building the kind of wealth that can pay for you plus ten or twelve others to fulfill that calling. Most importantly, you've bought yourself time to do it right. What's amazing, is you will be able to pass this abundance mindset on to your children, as well.

FROM THE DELI TO KENYA

Let me tell you about my fourteen year-old daughter, Amaya. As a part of our online school, we believe every child should experience a missions trip. So, the kids at Valor Global Online go on a trip each year. They work, raise money, and make it happen.

At Valor Global Online, we teach an abundance mindset. So my daughter Amaya decided she felt compelled to go on an upcoming trip to Kenya. So, I asked her how she would get there?

She replied, "I'm going to work for it and make it happen."

I told her, "That's what it's going to take."

My daughter knows how blessed she is. But, she works at a deli down the street from our house, clearing tables, sweeping, mopping, doing food takeout, and dishes—yes, at fourteen years old. Multiple times her boss has told me she's one of the best, hardest working employees on his staff of thirty.

You see, we believe teaching our kids a work ethic is crucial. Yes, they can ask for help. But they better be working harder than the help they're asking for. I'm a proud Papa to say, at the time of this writing, she's raised over $1,890 toward this trip. She has her separate savings, checking, and giving accounts. The point is, she's working like it depends on her and praying like it depends on God.

She's even in the middle of creating and designing a T-shirt to sell to support her trip. And all of the profits from the shirts will go towards her trip. She is paying for everything out of her pocket. She understands investing, but she also understands how to leverage her social media to promote the shirts and sell them online. Amaya is using her unique ability to go on this missions trip.

I know she's supposed to go to Kenya. She still has savings, is still giving, and I enjoy seeing her spend. I can't wait to see what miracles, blessing, and value God blesses the people of Kenya with through these students will be helping—and oh yeah, I hope and am praying for Amaya and all the kids to have life-changing experiences, too.

MISSIONAL MONEY MINDSET

One of the best things we can do for the current and coming generations is to shift them from a poverty mindset to one of ABUNDANCE. We should help them use technology and social media correctly and not try to avoid it, but teach them how to use it effectively to further their cause. Now, I think we can do for our kids what my parents did for me. They made me work for what I wanted and keep the focus on the mission, and not the missionary. Here's a detailed path to do that, and a guide to use video like I shared above.

Start by writing a letter or recording a video of the following. Email or Messenger is fine, as long as it's personalized to the sender. If it's generic on your social media that is great also, but the more personal it can become the better. While there can be similar parts of the video or message, it must build relational equity by inviting people into your why so they can be a part of your how.

This letter/video should give the recipient:

- *What the trip will be about*
- *Where and when it will be taking place*
- *Why you feel you should be going*
- *How much the trip will cost*
- *What you're personally putting in and paying for*
- *And how much you're trying to raise through work and donations*

It's very important you are upfront and honest that you need the money. Please do not cheapen this letter or video by moonlighting like it's a prayer card with the money as a simple bonus—because you and I both know it's not why you're sending the letter. Delta doesn't cash prayers and they won't fly you there on faith. They want the money. So let's get the money.

This letter or video could be followed up with a personal phone call or text within two to three days. But I'll give you a hint, if you are in relationship with the person, see them often, or are even friends on social media (which I hope you are), give them a like, bump, or "Hey what's up?" Just make sure you are building relational equity.

If you dare to test me on this, and if you or your kids do it right, I'm willing to bet you get a lot more money than you need for the trip—much before the total is even due. And you know what, for doing this right, working for it, and asking for it in the abundant way I just taught you, you deserve the extra. However, doing it this way will scare you. It will feel uncomfortable because it will demand you skill up and kick fear in the face by doing something outside of your comfort zone. But guess what, outside your comfort zone is where breakthrough, massive success, and money live.

My encouragement is, don't ask for something without going the extra mile. And parents, let's work hard on teaching this next generation social abundance skills, human interaction, and to get on video. That will serve them well in life far beyond the mission trip. This is something that will impact them for a lifetime just like a missions trip, and it will be an incredible educational experience that will start the missions trip off correctly because they earned it.

Remember it's the process that makes us. Let's not rob ourselves or our kids of the process of forming a missional money mindset.

BONUS RESOURCE

Approach raising money with an ABUNDANCE mindset. Get your free bonus resource, the **Abundant Fundraising Letter Template**, by visiting ChurchBoyToMillionaire.com

RELATIONAL EQUITY

——————

RELATIONAL EQUITY!!! Before reaching out to a friend or acquaintance about your business opportunity or next endeavor, asking for support, or just straight up asking for money for some unknown reason, first build some relational equity. At least tickle the relationship account and send a "What's up?" text or shoot off a "Hey, long time, no talk." Or just a good ole' fashioned, "How can I pray for you today?" I can't tell you how important it is to have had a conversation, have said hello, or even engaged in some social media interaction. It's important people feel valued and that you don't have an agenda. Unless you do?

"IF YOU ARE ADDING VALUE TO OTHERS, OWN YOUR ZONE, MAKE NO APOLOGIES FOR YOUR INCOME AND SUCCESS IN BUSINESS OR MINISTRY."

—@THEREALDOUGWOOD

#CHURCHBOYTOMILLIONAIRE

CHAPTER NINETEEN

WHY YOUR BUSINESS IS YOUR MINISTRY

I don't know what church you go to, or even if you do. But I'd like to talk to the people that do, the people with a pastor, volunteers, office staff, and musicians, who are pouring their blood, sweat, and tears into making your church stay and come alive. And I want to commend the nursery workers, parking-lot help, and greeters, because they show up day-in and day-out to keep your church afloat.

You see, I personally know of a church that does a lot of good in their community, but 19.2 percent of its members carry 81.3 percent of the entire financial load! And the same goes for those who serve. And we both know it's not the only one in this situation. This is freaking messed up! How have we gotten to this point? Now I'm going to say, your pastor needs your help. Yes there are things the church could be doing better. But that's not what I'm talking about here. It's important we understand that these people contributing and doing are giving their all. Many hands make light work.

I often chuckle to myself after the many events in and out of our home that we've hosted for people. The event is great. Community time is incredible. At the very end, it's always the same one or two people asking what they can do, how can they help, or better yet, just jump in. But then the other few people who participated follow me around asking to "pick my brain" and ask as I'm rolling up extension cords, mics, cleaning up bottles of water. I'm literally cleaning up after them while they watch me 🎥!

That is a poverty mindset and a habitual energy-stealer. We must be aware of this. We must do our part to serve our leaders. PRAY for them. PRAY for our military. PRAY for our senators. PRAY for our President. I didn't ask if you like or agree with them. I do believe it's our job to pray and support, and not be part of the problem. Your church, organization, or business needs us to step up and serve, not simply talk about the problems in America or our communities. Remember, unnecessary and highly emotional rants like these on social media are absolutely below-the-line, cause division, and never change anyone's mind anyways.

We must serve at a higher level. We must step into a higher calling. This is so important. It baffles me how many people miss this. Remember, ABUNDANCE is a MINDSET, not a number. I'm not telling you you need to give 10 percent. But if you sipped on free coffee in the last thirty days, you need to drop at least three dollars in the bucket next time it passes by ☺.

Now, I'm the first to say I'm sorry there are people on TV who abuse their power. Some TV preachers take money from vulnerable people, but I'm not talking about those people right now. I'm talking about the heart and the soul of your pastor. It's time to step up and give, to step up and serve, to level up, boss up, and pour your heart and soul into whatever organization of which you are a part.

BUSINESS OR MINISTRY?

This level of abundance applies both inside and outside the church building. Because I'm here to tell you, there is no line between business and ministry. You can do both all the time—and you should. But I didn't always understand this.

You see, I left ministry school in a confused state. I thought I had to choose between working in "ministry" and working in the "world." However, over time, I learned to meet in the middle, and discovered the ability to do both. The two collided. They are not mutually exclusive. You can—and should—be in *ministry* and *business*.

As my fellow graduates and I left our ministry school in 1999, most of my good friends went off to be senior pastors, some became kids pastors, another started a school assembly program, another took a job at his home church as a worship leader, and a few others stayed to train the next batch of students. But where does a guy who doesn't speak, preach, sing, act, or even know his calling go? What does he do?

Well, he goes home and starts a business with his father. And that's exactly what I did. I always said I wanted to be in ministry, but truth is it was because all my friends were passionate about it. I would have been getting into it for the wrong reasons. So, I chose the business and entrepreneurial world and some chose ministry. Now let's fast-forward twenty years to the fall of 2018.

One Sunday morning, I was in the mountains of Utah spending time with many other leaders at a three-day non-religiously affiliated retreat. It was about becoming a person of influence and the best leader possible. I spoke a couple times that weekend, sharing some wisdom, and truth— quite a few things that are in this book, in fact. But something interesting happened. I've always been very respectful of any stage I'm given, so I don't promote my personal spiritual views if it's a non-religious event. I don't slant any of my teachings to try to sway them.

First of all, I'd like to encourage anyone given a stage to honor it. You have every right to know and believe what you want to believe. But please understand, there are many faiths in your audiences, and I think we as speakers and leaders need to always respect the stage and the people who invited us. Part of this is only talking about what is appropriate, not pushing our personal or political beliefs onto them when it has nothing to do with our talks. Just like when I speak at many churches around the country, I don't share about my businesses. I may make a reference point as I live an integrated life, but it's simply inappropriate to abuse a stage for personal gain.

Why? I will never compromise who I am. I always strive to be respectful of any stage I stand upon. However, at the end of some of my conferences I do love seeing people that value many different religions, value the one true God, and who would like to spend some time on the last day, closing the retreat out in a time of honoring God together. As much as I respect the stage, I am always a husband, father, Christ follower, businessman, coach, entrepreneur, author, co-founder of an online school, minister and the list could go on. However, like I said before, I know which hat is appropriate and when.

So many times when I speak somewhere, people come up to me at the end to try and figure out my faith. They'll ask, "You're a Christ follower aren't you?" Now, they may use a different word. But the question is the same.

However, I don't like to simply be cast into a mold, spiritual affiliation, or religion. So, I ask, "How can you tell?"

They'll usually explain that there's something different about me. But, they're offended, asking, "Why didn't I share more of the Bible?"

MY CHURCH IN THE MOUNTAINS

You see, it's because I'd rather show them the love of Christ than inappropriately use a stage to simply tell them about it. This is my core belief about respecting the stage as leaders. And this same situation showed up in Utah, at the end of the retreat in the fall of 2018.

On this particular Sunday morning I was approached by an individual after I finished hosting an *optional* Bible-based morning devotional time following a weekend conference. This person said, "Wow Doug, that was an amazing time. You shared some powerful things, and so did the person you asked to speak. Have you ever considered becoming a pastor?"

I leaned forward. Then said, "Excuse me?" as if I didn't understand the question.

They repeated, "You would make a really good pastor, have you ever considered becoming one?"

Oh, I didn't need to hear it a second time. I knew full-well what they were asking. I was just giving them a chance to rethink their question. Social cue missed 😌.

I replied with a quizzical look, "I AM a full time pastor and this is my church."

I pointed to the people walking around us, and all of nature that we were surrounded by in those beautiful Utah mountains. This person looked at me with disappointment as if I wasn't understanding the question. I calmed him down, tapped him on the shoulder and said, "No, no my friend. I FULLY understand the question and let me explain. You see, when you are clear on your unique ability and purpose, you don't let four walls, a job, an income, or any limitations get in the way of your calling or your purpose."

Not too long ago, I realized that I'm called to help serve and add value to people. I make no apologies today that ministry and business have blended. You don't have to choose either-or. You don't have to choose between a massive income and a massive ministry. You can choose both. It looks different, sounds different. But if you are adding value at the highest level, you deserve to make a massive amount of income and you deserve great things.

So please, pastor, if you can afford a BMW, and you're working hard, please start driving it. Seriously, you deserve it and should be driving whatever you want, can afford, and whatever makes you happy. (Now I hope you don't have a reserved parking space with your name on it though 😝, but we'll talk about that later.)

Here's the truth, whether you drive a Kia, a Honda, a Lexus, or an Escalade, drive it with confidence. Pimp that thing out if you want 👊. Be you. I drive nice cars because of how they make me feel and how I show up with excellence. People can get over themselves and their own opinions of you. People who are going to talk about it will talk about you anyway, so give them something good to talk about.

Anyone judging doesn't know the full story. If you're helping make this world a better place, own your zone, and get it done. Then make no apologies for your income, success in *business, and in ministry.*

STOP SACRIFICING PEOPLE FOR "STRATEGY"

Remember . . . your best and most relevant currency is the AUTHENTIC YOU! People can smell if you're a fake and have an agenda from a mile away. Be authentic in both your connections and praise of another. Never sacrifice being the AUTHENTIC YOU, or making a HEARTFELT connection for "a gimmick, a strategy, or an algorithm." Thea and I took an oath to ourselves years ago that we would never sacrifice people for strategy. It simply doesn't work, and it's a mistake I see many people make.

"**THE** HIGHEST **VALUED CURRENCY** EXCHANGED **TODAY IS YOU GETTING** REAL **AND BEING** AUTHENTIC."

———

—@THEREALDOUGWOOD
@CHURCHBOYTOMILLIONAIRE

CHAPTER TWENTY

LEADERSHIP CURRENCY

I've learned some things over the past few years about something I call AUTHENTIC LEADERSHIP. It is a new breed of leader who focuses on relational equity. You see, I had to unlearn some leadership styles that were relevant a decade or more ago but are now irrelevant and could cause confusion and hurt in organizations.

So yes, I have gone against the grain of what a leader is supposed to be. I have gone against much of what I saw growing up, or even observe in many organizations today. And you know what it is? It's a lack of authentic leadership that, though not necessarily "fake," is focused on telling you what to do. It's a positional mindset that alludes to a mastery of every area of life, telling you how you should think, feel, and behave. But there is a complete lack of these leaders opening their own lives up to how they are *still doing it.* The TRUTH is that the most RELEVANT LEADERS today join the people they lead in learning and growing. They model this leadership on the frontlines.

Here's what that may look like for you: Start giving people a window into your life, your thoughts, what you deal with, what some of your personal goals are, what type of expectations you set for yourself, what your daily challenges are, and identify what you go through on a day-to-day basis to practice what you preach. Starting this process will be an incredible entry point into creating trust, and soon, a very healthy, relevant, relatable authentic, and thriving culture in your organization.

I'll give you a couple of examples from working with many people in many different organizations over the years.

CEO/Sales Manager

The next time you're in a sales meeting, pick up the phone and get a live client on the line. Show your team the questions you want them to ask. Show them how to overcome objections. And model everything else they can do. After you're off, let them know what your intention was, and what you would've done differently if you had the chance. There is always something new to be learned. Your team will respect you more, and will be able to learn from you more. Remember, you're not perfect, and neither are they. And then, sales manager, if they're supposed to make twenty sales phone calls, why don't you sit there and make twenty with them?

Pastor

Pastors, I dare you to do Facebook Live this week and share a three-to-five-minute message from your home or your car. Tell your people how you're using your time and making the most of that day count. How are you implementing what you taught from your sermon the previous Sunday? How are you facing the same life challenges they are? And most importantly, what actions are YOU taking to live out what you teach?

RELEVANT LEADERS SHARE THEIR JOURNEY

The point is, people have been starving—I mean starving—for this type of person or leader for years. I know Thea and I spend a lot of time wondering if we are the only ones that deal with marriage stuff, getting on the same page as spouses, how to parent better, or thinking we're the only ones who don't have it figured out?

Others of you might be wondering if you are the only one missing your quota. Or, are we the only parents dealing with a bedtime routine for our two-year-old? Am I the only one who can't remember what the pastor said last Sunday? We think these people in leadership, our bosses and pastors, don't deal with stuff like we do.

For me, I felt like I was never getting clear answers. Sometimes I was pointed to a book, but I felt isolated and confused. I even thought I was disqualified from being a leader or growing. Why? Because I seemed to be the only one that couldn't figure out the *easy* stuff.

Can you relate to this? Or was I the only one? I want you to know, that Doug Wood, yes @TheRealDougWood, Mr. Church Boy to Millionaire, entrepreneur, coach, husband, dad, or whatever else you want to call me, is still on this journey of figuring life out, too.

As I'm writing this, I'm still trying to get to a healthier weight. I am currently doing everything I can to not look at my phone before bedtime and the moment I wake up. My workouts have been on and off this year— though they're headed in the right direction. My relationship with Thea is incredible, however, we just had a pretty intense conversation a couple nights ago, and I owed her an apology for something I said. My three kids are growing up so fast, and I'm trying to figure out how to give better one-on-one time to each of them. (Feel free to ask me how that's going the next time you see me.) But I will also tell you, writing this book is not easy. I've sat here in tears multiple times the last few nights fighting for the words, wondering and doubting if this is going to be a total dud.

Speaking of nights, I was up working on this last night until 2 a.m. because I'm under a deadline, and I'm nervous as hell that I'm not going to finish this book. Or that I'll take a shortcut and cheapen the content because I'm rushing it to get it done to meet the deadline. But I won't let that happen. I'm committed to this. I'm committed to you. Give me grace and I'll return it to you. Remember, we're on this journey together.

The point is, I'm dealing with all of it too. Here's the truth: we are all going through it—but too few are talking about it. Of course, use good wisdom as there is a right and a wrong time to talk about something, depending on the situation.

Look, with anything you do, it's important you are talking about how you are getting through it, how you did it, and what you did to overcome. When you do, people will gravitate toward you. They will connect first. That will lead to trust, which will create respect. Remember, people want to know how you get through things and you will be a voice of confirmation and clarity assisting them to get through it as well.

Simply by doing this, without even knowing it, they have just given you a whole new level of permission to lead them. Because you are now an authentic leader. They see you are shoulder-to-shoulder with them, and you are now in the process of building (or rebuilding) trust and loyalty in your organization.

My friends, what will happen next, if you dare to test me on this, is breakthrough and freedom. And it will take place while connecting at authentic levels: human-to-human and spirit-to-spirit. How? All by giving them a small window into your life.

TODAY'S RELATIONAL CURRENCY

You must understand, AUTHENTICITY is a form of CURRENCY, just like the $100 bill in your pocket. It will buy you something, won't it? Everyone knows the value of money. Very few people understand that authenticity in our current culture has a much higher value than that Benjamin 💵.

I got to where I am today by applying this law. If you want to know the truth, I have caught hell from a few leaders, pastors, and everyday Joes who feel the need to give me their opinions on some of the things I talk about publicly. Why? Because they are not willing to be AUTHENTIC. It goes against their fifteen-year-old, outdated leadership style. Or even if it's not outdated, it's just something they wouldn't do themselves. That's OK, I have just found that the many people I talk to are crying out for more relevance. Because on the flip side, I get tons of messages each week thanking me about being open and honest about what it takes to be a husband,

EMOTIONALLY HIJACKED VS EMOTIONALLY AWARE

Emotionally Hijacked: When we don't even realize we're lying to ourselves about a drama-filled situation, or acting out in negative emotion. People around us see it, and maybe even try to say something, but ultimately don't because they value the relationship and business.

Emotionally Aware: When we are consciously aware of what is going on around and within us. Whether it be good or bad emotions, staying in control of ourselves, maintaining an awareness of others, and seeing any situation for what it is. Choosing to observe, feel, and acknowledge emotions (our own and other people's), but acting in alignment with the reason, goal, structure, or outcome we desire.

father, leader, businessman, and coach—on what it takes to contend for a marriage, on the hustle required to build a business. I simply share my life, wins, and challenges with those who choose to follow.

Friends, never forget this: You ARE a CURRENCY. You have a value. You want to increase it? Increase your authenticity. Remember this, the HIGHEST valued currency and EXCHANGE today is you getting real, thus building TRUST in your organization. Watch your stock rise. What would it be like to become a Fortune 500 organization?

ASKING PERMISSION TO GIVE ADVICE?

Authentic leaders develop relationships with people who then give you permission to speak into their lives. Positional leaders (the old way of leading) simply tell others how to live their lives. They lead from *position*, not from *permission*. And it simply comes off as controlling.

The fastest way to ruin a relationship and push someone away is to tell someone how to live their life when you are not currently in their LIFE— meaning an influential relationship with someone.

If you don't know their current why, heart, passion, hurt, desire, place of pain, or purpose, then I suggest being very careful when giving advice when not asked. Here's the truth, just because someone works for you, is a family member, is on staff with you, or is within your computer system, does not mean you have an open door. If you feel so led and have a suggestion for someone that you really care about, ALWAYS ask permission before offering your Wise Counsel. Then, only give it if they are OPEN to hearing your thoughts because they believe you can help them.

My friends, please be careful. As leaders, we are dealing with people's real lives, hearts, and sensitivities. When people lay their heads on their pillows at night, hurtful comments and opinions given without love or relationship can cause real damage. They can even cause growth and production to stall, or cause them to question everything while causing major confusion. Authentic leaders focus on developing influential friendships, and ask more questions than they give answers.

THE FLAWED EXPERT

Anyone who knows me knows I'm a flawed expert in many areas (including my grammar on my Facebook posts! Thank you to my amazing friend Jordan for making sure I don't have too many run-on sentences or typos 😋. However, because it's my book, I'll see to it you will find something!)

Actually, when people correct my grammar or punctuation, and point it out on public social media to me, I usually unfollow them. (Now if they send it to me in private like a friend would, that's different.) Now, I don't unfollow someone because they are wrong, but by pointing out my flaws on a public forum, it shows me where they invest their obsessive energy. I am a flawed individual. I am in pursuit of becoming the best version of myself. I'm aware of my flaws and am trying to improve. I'm working on my grammar and spelling. I graduated high school with a C- average, I got a D in English, and have zero college education. But I wrote this book and you are reading it. Because the truth is, I focus on my strengths and get help in my weaknesses, but don't let them stop me.

I try to live my life out loud and show the love of my Jesus who lives inside me. I work hard and DO the HEART work more than just talk about it. I try to act more than I talk about what I'm doing, because I'd rather show you than tell you. It seems like a lot of people spend their time getting ready just to get ready! I spent enough years telling my friends and family what I was going to do. Instead, now I just do it, then let the data and results do the talking.

This also means that authenticity, to me, is posting content when I feel inspired to post. And not posting when I don't. Because there are some days I just can't do it. I'm sorry I don't have it in me to copy and paste, set up an automated service, or manufacture some Photoshopped picture of myself and how great life might be that day. It may not actually be that great that day—you will know the rest because I share AUTHENTICALLY.

Authentic leaders do this because they're focused on meeting people where they're at. You see, I love traveling and meeting new people on their turf. Until Donald Trump, Abraham Lincoln was the only President to spend more time out of the White House, than in it. Whether you agree with either of them, that isn't the point. The point is, they met people on their turf because they are confident in who they are, and understand others are more comfortable on their turf, in their home, business, or local coffee shop, and it's about going to people versus asking people to come only to us.

Where are people today? They're on social media. They're on their devices ▐ , just like where many of you are right now. You see, I'm coming to you. I went to great lengths to ensure I was bringing you this message in a way you could understand it and wanted to receive it.

Let me tell you, it's been quite an inconvenience trying to publish on all platforms simultaneously. But that's my worry, not yours. Because leaders meet people where they're at, and they don't ask them to adapt to their leadership or communication style.

I am beginning to learn how to manage my energy. I know when to turn it on, and when to turn it off and fill my own cup. It's still a work in progress. Even though I'm nine years into the journey, I still have a long way to go. I'm not telling you I have it all figured out. Instead, I'm figuring it out WITH you, and simply sharing my experience along the way. But the one thing you can count on, everything you read here or listen to will always be me—the authentic me.

YOU'RE NOT GOING CRAZY

Some of you love me. Others of you are still trying to make me more palatable and figure me out. Honestly, don't waste time doing that. I'm just here to say it the way I wish someone would've told me ten years ago. My prayer 🙏 for this book has been to help you think beyond your safety and comfort zones, or possibly even open you up to some closed-off areas of thinking that were relevant years ago but aren't any longer. But now, I've given you the freedom that the thoughts you've had in your head could be true, even accurate. And no, my friend, you're not going crazy. Like me, you're on the journey, evolving and growing. It sounds to me like you're chasing the best version of yourself.

I bet by now you are seeing ideas to tap even deeper into the REAL YOU and sharing more parts of the REAL YOU. I know for a fact people are going to appreciate you sharing your life experiences. They will love having an authentic connection with you through your current experiences. While this will bring them so much freedom, you will also find freedom because you will be so relatable to yourself and others.

As for me, *@TheRealDougWood*, I'm unapologetic. I'm FREE TO BE me.

A LEADER SHOWS UP

———

A leader doesn't make excuses or let their team down because of personal issues or emotions. If they're having a bad day or life situation, and they can't show up well for their team, it is 100 percent their responsibility. Leaders don't put that on their team.

They boss up and do what they have to do, get the job done and be a pro. Nobody wants to follow someone who is inconsistent, and always up-and-down, because this doesn't affect just them, it affects everyone around them. Real leaders are pros, because they know they have to show up even when they don't feel like it to be taken seriously!

"**TRUE LEADERS OF TODAY DON'T SIT OVER YOU, THEY SIT WITH YOU.**"

———

CHAPTER TWENTY ONE

LEADERS SIT WITH YOU, NOT "OVER" YOU

Let me tell you about the first time I introduced myself to Thea. How she eventually married me is proof of God working absolute miracles. You know, things like turning water into wine, making man out of a pile of dirt, and getting Thea to marry me 😜.

In 1999, I was a second-year student in Master's Commission, and Thea was a first-year. I'd been travelling for a few weeks doing school assemblies with the road team. When I came back into town, I met up with the small team I was supposed to be leading but hadn't been because of the travel. Now, bear in mind, I had never met any of these twelve people.

At this point, I was also feeling good about myself, Mr. Hotshot, second-year, just back from the road. I'll never forget meeting a few others, but of course, Thea soon stood out. And the very first time I met her, I said the words I would love to have back!

I said, "Hi Thea, I'm Doug and I am your leader!"

Let that set in. A person you'd never met before telling you he is your leader 🙄. But here's the truth, that's the way leadership worked back then. You lead with title and position, not with influence. Now, if this happened today, I would hope those twelve people would walk out and tell me to go pound sand.

I didn't know them, and they didn't know me. I had no idea what needs, desires, or goals they had. That should've been a clue that I shouldn't come in swinging with a title. How can I lead someone if I don't know what they want?

It chuckles me to this day when people I don't know leave me voicemails, give their title (like it's a big deal), and ask me to call them back. I don't know them and their title means nothing to me. There is no relationship there to ask me to do anything. It's just so important, my friends, that we fully understand that:

1. Our titles mean nothing to people until we have done something for them.
2. If we earn our title, that means we are in relationship and production-level leadership.
3. Our titles aren't as important as we think, and often they're there to inflate our egos.

I'm simply sharing a mindset that has caused much confusion and hurt in many organizations. So, let's get into the problem of positional leadership and how it's harming our organizations today. And then, if you shift and make the changes I suggest below, how it will have dramatic, positive impact in your organization.

POSITIONAL LEADERSHIP

Gone are the days of positional leadership, or should we just call it LEADER-SLIP 😄. Because I see many leaders slip by leading the same way they were even just a few years ago. I have discovered that, if you are still leading the in *same old way*, your organization, business, or church is reflecting it.

You can either face it, or run from it, but here's the truth:

- The leaders of today are INFLUENTIAL and AUTHENTIC— not positional.

- The leaders of today are doing it "with" you—not just telling you what they used to do.
- The leaders of today are in the trenches mentoring you, guiding you, on the phones with you, on video, and spending time on the front lines with you and your organization.
- The leaders of today are not leading from the fear of losing you.
- The leaders of today are not comparing you to someone else and making you feel less valuable than them.
- The leaders of today want something for you, not something from you.

I don't care how big your organization is. If you are not on the front lines (at least sometimes), yet still call yourself a leader, have a sign, title, name tag, or reserved parking space with your name on it, then with all due respect, step aside and let the next leaders rise up. People are starving for TRUTH, AUTHENTICITY, and truly INFLUENTIAL LEADERS. They want someone to show them the way, develop them, and spend time with them.

Of course they have to do the work—but as leaders we must do our part to make sure we are meeting and leading this new generation of world-changers. They just want a mentor, coach, or a pastor to guide them, lead them, help them develop, and even send them out if needed. They do not want a wet blanket thrown on their dreams or fresh ideas. (Which, honestly, are probably innovative and could spark massive growth in your organization.)

At times, I have had many people introduce themselves to me in what I feel is a very awkward way. For a frame of reference, the first thing they tell me is who or what organization they "sit under." Usually they are referencing a pastor, boss, leader, or organization. Let me be clear: LEADERS of today don't sit over you, they sit WITH you, and EVERYONE is EQUAL!

Oh sure, there are systems, healthy hierarchies, and order in place that make sense for structure and organization. However, leaders, please hear me, don't say you are "over" anyone. Because you're not. And everyone else, you are not "under" anyone. Yes, honor and respect is a good thing and we need to give honor where it's due, but don't put these people on pedestals and eat at their feet. That's just weird and unhealthy. Honor and respect are appropriate when a leader has done great things for you and modeled great leadership, but pedestal worship is a scary place to be, and that's where people get hurt.

Five years ago, I read the leadership book that was most influential in changing the health of my organization, John Maxwell's *5 Levels of Leadership*. It's absolutely profound, and should be consumed and applied three to four times. Because I read it over and over and over again and realized what level of leader I really was, it transformed the way I saw and pursued leadership. In the book, he shares the five levels of leadership, or influence, you can be on with someone else:

1. **Position:** People follow you because they have to.
2. **Permission:** People follow you because they want to.
3. **Production:** People follow you because of what you have done for the organization.
4. **People Development:** People follow you because of what you have done for them.
5. **Pinnacle:** People follow you because of who you are and what you represent.

You see, the higher you go, the greater value you have given to the person. The best leaders win respect and loyalty because of their character and how they've served their followers. And did you notice that the lowest level of leadership comes from a title? Our titles are worthless because positional leadership simply doesn't work anymore.

So, I understand that some of you reading this have come up against this type of CONTROL and POSITIONAL leadership, and your income, job, or position is riding on it. And you're saying, Doug, what do I do?

First, I am honestly sorry. This is jacked up, as there are still some leaders that haven't transformed into INFLUENTIAL LEADERS. Or maybe bad leadership was passed on to them from the previous generation, and they don't even know that what they're doing is a problem.

I truly believe people and leaders are doing the best they can with what they know. I don't believe leaders are trying to be controlling, do a poor job, make you feel bad, sit over you, or throw their title around. I'm not saying this to make excuses for them, but we naturally model what has been taught to us. And it's likely they don't have anyone in their truth corner giving them wise counsel. Worse, they may be closed off to it and are unwilling to change.

For me, this is where I had to unlearn some things. In fact, I even had to untangle this from my own leadership. However, I'll be completely honest with you, if you are currently dealing with an extremely positional, ego-, or title-driven leader, then you are either at a place you can stay and continue on the path you're on, or you might be in a place where you're ready to call it and not accept being under the dictatorship of someone treating you this way and disrespecting you.

I don't know where you're at, but I'd encourage you to exercise self-respect and have a hard conversation if you think it would improve the situation. Or, it may be time to leave altogether. I understand this may be financially challenging, so please use wisdom during this process. But how much longer can you be treated the way you are—especially from someone who acts one way certain days of the week, then completely different on others?

Just understand, these leaders can be in any industry or organization. But, they generally have the same traits:

- A reserved parking space. YES, my favorite because they are super important! And they're way too busy to walk twenty more steps than everyone else.

- They most likely introduce themselves by their title: PASTOR BILL versus just Bill when you don't even go to their church. Or their Facebook or Instagram handle tells you what they are and how important they might be ☺.
- They often keep you on guard, or on edge, around them.

Have you ever noticed you can't quite relax around individuals like this? It's not because they're operating at a higher frequency. (Because people operating at a higher frequency are often the most genuine, authentic, and kind people you'll ever meet. AND they often have massive positions at massive organizations.) My guess is the leaders I described haven't honestly asked how you, your kids, and your family are doing in a very long time. In fact, some leaders of this type might not even know your kids' names.

Now, the several hundred people I work with often, please give me some grace. But I think you're getting my point. Even a genuine, "Hello!", "How are you?", "Any vacations this summer?" is great. Just a genuine conversation from a boss to an employee—human to human.

CONTROLLING LEADERSHIP

Being a coach for the last few years, it's interesting how I've gotten several messages from church staff, sometimes even those who work part-time, that read: "Doug, what should I do? My pastor will no longer allow me to post things about my side hustle on my personal Facebook page."

Hold up, wait a minute. What?! Let me get this right. You're telling me you work for a church that pays you just over the poverty line (because they told me their income), and then they tell you where you can, and cannot, work to improve your family's income and life? All while trying to control what you say?

My dear goodness. If you want to LIVE under this type of controlling leadership then by all means do so. Who am I to say you shouldn't? Do whatever you want. In fact, I encourage you to do what's best for you as this is a FREE country. However, there comes a point where organized religion can cross a boundary and it becomes "control my people religion." Honestly, it's dangerous to be near this type of stuff.

You will at first feel confused, questioning yourself. You will feel like it's your fault and you just need to "submit," as you have been taught to respect authority and not cause disruptions. Then you'll start feeling like you're the only one, isolated, and wondering if you might be crazy. No brother or sister, you are not the crazy one. However you ARE in a crazy situation. And you may need to step back and look at it from a higher vantage point. In fact, it might be time to consider not staying aboard the crazy train any longer.

By all means, I understand how side hustles and internet businesses have caused destruction in some churches or organizations. However, in the cases of controlling leadership that I'm referring to, there was no trouble. Instead, it was simply controlling behavior driven by the fear of loss. Or by a story of something that had happened in friends' churches years ago in the MLM movement.

So leaders, my encouragement to you is to never shut down someone's passion or unique ability just because it's different, social-media-driven, or you don't understand it. Controlling leadership forces people to work at a coffee shop or a bookstore for their secondary income, because it's familiar. But authentic leadership allows freedom and encourages abundance.

My friends, we are all on a different journey of life. However, in speaking and coaching thousands of people around the country over the last few years, I have definitely learned: we are all going through the same stuff, we are all questioning the same things, and we are all praying for similar things in life, marriage, family, finances, and faith. I think it's important we all stop being so politically correct and filtering our lives. Let's show more of what is going on behind the scenes and how we are getting through the day-to-day.

We all have value to share with each other. Let's not devalue what we all do well. What's very basic to you is mind-blowing to me. We can and should be learning from each other as we become authentic people and leaders who raise our relationship equity.

WHY YOUR TITLE IS WORTHLESS

If a leader needs to remind you that *they* are in charge, they are no longer the leader! Influential leaders or bosses don't need to remind their people of their titles. Their influence and example speak for themselves, and people want to follow them.

"LEADERS, IF WE WANT TO GROW, WE'VE GOT TO LEARN TO LET GO."

—@THEREALDOUGWOOD

CHAPTER TWENTY TWO

ARE WE CREATING LEADERS OR FOLLOWERS?

The truth is, some people honestly want followers. Followers are easy; they do whatever we say. They're fans. They tell us how great we are. Even though they often suck the energy out of us, there's a part of us that likes it because we look like the hero.

The challenging thing is, we have no freedom. We can make decisions fast because we have a team of yes-men and nobody will challenge us. The problem is, when we step away from the office for a week or two each year for our vacations, we're either attached to the phone or we shut the thing down knowing we'd come home to a complete mess.

If you're someone who wants more followers, this chapter is not for you. Let me tell you about a time six years ago when I wanted to build LEADERS and not followers. But it wasn't going to happen until I got the obstacle out of the way—and the obstacle was me.

THE OBSTACLE OF EGO

My friend Bekah was our neighbor in Hillsboro, Oregon. She and her husband started in our coaching business with us years ago. They were, and are still, incredible friends and leaders. They make huge impact in their community, and now across the country and, very soon, the world. After a few

years of working closely with them in mentoring and coaching, we didn't need to spend much time mentoring with them anymore. Honestly, they were growing and becoming incredible leaders and were taking the business further than we were.

The ultimate truth behind the whole thing was, their organization made up a large part of ours. You see, we always did mutual events, Christmas parties, business dinners, gatherings, and trainings together. Deep down inside, I loved it. They brought their team and shared in some training. But the truth was, I knew their team was growing at a much more accelerated rate than the rest of our team. I was aware of this, but I didn't want to totally admit it. Being totally honest now, there was a big part of me that wanted to keep control and everything looking good on the outside because it inflated my ego and made me look good. The truth was me trying to stay in control was halting their growth.

The question I had to ask myself was, is there enough room on the stage for people who are better at it than me, even if I had helped lead them? Could I step aside so they could grow and then everyone else around them would, too? Well, at the time no, I could not, and here is what happend.

Bekah called me one day and said, "Hey Doug, we decided we'd like to host a team party on our own at the event coming up."

I'll never forget, I was driving in the car and thought to myself, oh crap, this will expose me. And then I uttered the words I to this day regret: "You CAN'T do that!"

Meanwhile, understand she was NOT an employee of mine. She could do whatever she'd like.

She replied, "Excuse me?"

"We have something planned already," I said, "so we need to do this event together."

"Well," she said in an even sweeter tone, "we'd like to do something on our own and learn with our team and bring up some new voices."

Then I said the words: "Who gave you permission to have your own team party?"

I want to park right there and admit what was really going on in my mind. If Bekah took her team, it exposed my team for what it was. It struck serious fear in me that I was being outgrown and undervalued. But I was strokin' my ego—and this exact ego is what held my organization and me up. But, if I'm even more honest, it was a habit loop of mine. If you look back on every business or ministry I had ever run, there had never been enough room for more than me on the stage or taking the lead.

This was a painful lesson that day, as I fought so hard to hold onto my ego and leadership POSITION. The truth was, the "leader" needed to step aside and let the people who were ready go, grow, and emerge.

Now, since that day, I have since taken full responsibility for my fear and ego. Thank you to my now very good friend Bekah for giving me grace in that season as I was learning a painful lesson in ego. I also realized I had to let go of trying to make a "Wood Team" mentality instead of a leadership mentality. I chose to start creating more leaders and fewer followers.

Leaders, if we want to grow, we've got to learn to let go.

True freedom comes in duplication of our skills into another. Leaders grow leaders; egos need followers. Empowering and letting go of competent, up-and-coming leaders who think for themselves, operate with autonomy, generate innovative ideas, and multiply themselves.

TRUE LEADERS DON'T CREATE MORE FOLLOWERS, THEY CREATE MORE LEADERS!!!

True leaders win people over, build and develop them, and then send them to duplicate the process with others. They do this without attachment, mind games, or ego. And they never try to hold them back. Those who only attract followers might have some nice friends, numbers may look good, but they really never develop into leaders themselves. Usually, they depend upon their *leaders* for the answer, pulling them down in the process.

Soon after that, followers start to feel that they can never compare, accomplish, become, or duplicate what that leader has done. Usually, this is because the organization lacks a growth mindset, starting with the leaders themselves.

Also, if people who lead have a co-dependent leadership relationship with their followers, their identity only comes from their people liking or always needing them. That's not building freedom for the leader, or empowering their team, and it's certainly not people development. Again, it's often feeding an ego.

The leader has only created himself or herself a job in which every decision goes through them. This leaves "followers" who never feel empowered. They only feel distant, frustrated, and will eventually leave. Or they may just disappear because comparative reality, shame, embarrassment, or a lack of results or production finally sets in. Honestly, they realize this train is one that'll never stop if they don't get off. Also, let's not forget to mention, this type of leadership style wears leaders down as well!

My encouragement to LEADERS is to keep your ego in check. Make sure the VISION and PURPOSE are clear for your organization. Make sure your identity is not wrapped up in being the hero. Make sure you empower people to think and act for themselves. And if nothing else, make sure you, your system, ministry, or whatever you do is duplicable.

If you do things right, people you help develop will respect who you are, and what you have done. Why? Because they will know that they will—and can—duplicate who you are and what you've done, even if it takes a little longer. And hopefully, they can do it bigger and better than you ever did while seeking you out for occasional mentorship or guidance.

If that happens, you now know how to win followers, develop them as leaders, and send them out to duplicate.

WHAT ARE YOU TRYING TO BUILD?

My real question, my friends, is what are you trying to build? Are you in competition with yourself, with someone else, with someone on the internet, or with another organization or business across town? Only you can answer those questions. Part of building a healthy business or ministry is confirming that the organization is pure in its purpose.

In today's world, I'm seeing more and more in hero-based organizations, where it has become more about the leader than the mission. You can probably think of plenty of leaders like this right now, but the important thing is that if you allow you or your organization to slip into hero worship, it will become more and more about the numbers, attendance, or volume than the mission. Really, it will devolve into complete mission drift and became all about income, fame, and notoriety.

See, these types of organizations are outstanding because they are generally led by a gifted communicator. The problem is, there's no room on the stage except for that person—and everybody knows it. This can be exhausting for the hero. The hero likes the attention in the beginning. But the slippery slope is if that leader needs a break, vacation, or sabbatical, they have transferred very few skills, or failed to raise up many influential leaders, and the organization can implode.

My friends, it is our duty to guard ourselves from this. To constantly examine and take the temperature of our organization, to ask ourselves,

"Is this becoming more about me, or this mission, impact, and business we're trying to create?"

Also, there are some really, really, REALLY quality young men and women in your church or organization that could seriously use some mentorship right now. They would love some one-on-one time with you once in awhile, and there's somebody that would love a shot next Sunday. Put them in coach, they're ready. You know it. They just need someone to speak life into them and guide them and coach them up.

HERO OR LEADER?

Hero, just know that these men and women aren't going to do it as good as you—not even close. But give them a shot, some constructive coaching, then another shot. The bottom line is, how else are they going to get ready unless they get thrown into the fire, the same way you did.

Let's prepare them. Let's step off the stage a little more often. Let's make sure this next generation is ready to take over—or better yet, to be sent out. And if there is some ego in you (which there will be—we all have it), you will know you helped them get their start. Because you put them in, coach, and today it's time to coach them up. Now go, take a few of your followers dying to be leaders. Lead with EXCELLENCE, INTEGRITY, and show them what AUTHENTIC LEADERSHIP looks like.

If you're worried you might be developing a hero brand—or serving under one—here are five practical questions you should constantly answer:

1. *Do you need to kill your ego?*
2. *Are you willing to give away your platform?*
3. *Do you seek to develop others more than promote yourself?*
4. *Is there enough room on the stage for others?*
5. *Will the whole thing fall apart if you leave?*

STOP COUNTING THE LIKES 👍

In a world of hero brands, of obsessive "like" counting, of constantly asking "How many people attended my event?" or "How big is my church, organization, ministry, or business?" there is a more authentic way to lead. Today, the true definition of growth is all about your ability to DUPLI-CATE YOURSELF and your systems—and it is the best way to reach the masses!!!

Leaders, I encourage you to get away from number-counting and get into people's lives. Share your good times and bad times. Share what you've learned and what you would do better—or differently—if you had to do it over. This makes a lasting impact on your "followers" because they can then become LEADERS. Of course, if you're scared that they will "leave you" then that is just called an ego and operating out of fear 😕. But, I will save that for another book 😛.

Be great today and go DEVELOP someone. Everyone reading this is leading someone. Maybe it's your kids, spouse, an employee—it really doesn't matter. Large or small, you are in a leadership position.

So my friends, are you building LEADERS or FOLLOWERS?

BUILD LEADERS, NOT FOLLOWERS

A true leader is not the one with the most followers, but the one who duplicates himself, creating more leaders. Remember, having followers feels good for a while and serves the ego. But leaders serve others and the world rather than themselves. And that's where duplication and freedom take place for you and increases your impact on humanity.

"DREAMS TAKE WORK."

─────────

─@THEREALDOUGWOOD

CHAPTER TWENTY THREE

STOP SELLING HYPE AND HOPEIUM

In the last twelve years, I've attended over 100 conferences. Some of faith, and others not. It seems like many of the faith conferences I've been to (and will still occasionally peek my head into) are one to three days filled with little more than HYPE and HOPEIUM. Meaning, we get pumped up with emotions and beliefs that something great is about to happen in our lives or faith journeys, only to walk out, and within twenty-four hours, be in the same situation with the same bank account and the same marriage that we walked in with. We get left to figure out the "how-to" on our own. Both the speaker and the conference move on, but we stay the same, praying for the same miracles. Go figure . . . I'm sorry, but this is not right 🙍.

At the same time, some personal growth conferences I've been to seem focused on selling stuff while delivering very few details on how to actually grow during the conference itself. By all means, I'm a huge fan of sales, however, I believe one should only sell more stuff AFTER delivering the value a conference promised in the first place. I'll be honest with you, I believe the world is crying out for honest, authentic leaders to step up and deliver raw, real, and simple how-to content with daily action plans.

I can also say that out of all these 100-plus conferences, I have learned something from every one of them (and I don't regret going). So it's important that we always stay open-minded to learning and growing, concentrating more on eating the fish, and spitting out the bones. However, we must always make sure we're giving people more fish and fewer bones.

So leaders, if you are going to tell people to have BIG DREAMS or to START DREAMING AGAIN, then you better make it crystal clear they need an even bigger ACTION plan to turn it into reality. Big dreams take a lot of work.

In fact, you had better make sure that YOU spend more time assisting them, showing them, coaching them, and guiding them, helping them see what activities to do, the order to do them in, and understand what it's going to take to accomplish that DREAM. Otherwise, I feel that their failed dreams are on you. You sold it without an instruction manual, system, a book, a worksheet, or some kind of four-to-six week follow-up workshop.

Otherwise, if you don't help them achieve it, you are selling them a pipe dream. And whether you know it or not, dreams are actually impossible until the action plan is implemented. I've discovered that dreams will be dead within a week of people returning to their normal, oscillating structures of life. Oscillating structures are patterns or habits we fall back into that prevent us from taking key, sustainable steps forward toward our desires or goals. It's easy to get hyped up on the hopeium of a new day, a new goal, a new week. But soon, the hype wears off and without a new, advancing structure, we find ourself back in the same mess where we started.

"START DREAMING AGAIN"

Back in the day, I paid money to go to many conferences telling me to start dreaming again. However, many are now being given away for free at local churches. And remember, if something is free, what could the value be, or the upsell to lay down and "Invest money you don't have in someone else's dream so yours can come true"?

Personally, I have a huge issue with this. How is it right to guilt (or manipulate) people into debt to expand your building fund? I personally know of way too many stories about good people getting caught up in the emotions of HYPE and HOPEIUM. It's causing confusion, hurt, and even causing people to give up on God because it's a path of broken dreams. The challenging part with anyone or anything who tells me to dream again is they often don't tell me HOW to "do" the dream—or even get the dream started. I was always left to go home and figure out that part on my own. And within forty-eight hours, I was stuck in my own crap again, not knowing how to get out except I had even less money than I showed up with.

The days of selling HYPE and HOPEIUM must come to an end. People want the brutal and honest truth. They don't just want to be *told* something is possible, or get pitched on more products or services to buy, they want to be told HOW to make it possible for them with a step-by-step action plan that should be INCLUDED with the price of the conference

Speaking of the how, in Chapter 2 we took a deep dive into what do we want, why do we want it, and how to break that process down into measurable action steps. I'm not going to break the entire process down here, but I encourage you to apply the same principles to any dream, vision, and goal you have had.

Please, my friends, never stop dreaming. You must totally own your current reality and where you're at in relation to the dream. Then, get help from someone who has done what you want to accomplish. They will help you define a daily, weekly, and monthly action plan.

SUMMER CAMP SYNDROME

I'll close this chapter with taking us all back to summer camp. For me, it was the mountain-top experiences of Camp Davidson in central Oregon. Do you remember how amazing summer camp was? . . . for many reasons—and I know what you're thinking 😉.

However, I've always had some of the most unique and incredible mountain-top experiences with my Creator at summer or winter camps. And today, I still have similar experiences at conferences. But in the past, I'd come home and within a day that summer camp experience felt so far away.

Now, Thea and I have come up with something to COMMIT to when we go to conferences. When we are in the emotion and feeling and excitement of that conference, we can feel new ideas, new dreams, God speaking, and the things that must change now. So we always commit to the ACTION, create a plan, and even take the first ACTION before leaving that conference.

We have done this for the last nine years. We always leave with a worksheet, napkin sketch, a written plan—and always before the wheels of the airplane touch down at home.

We fully know the scope of what we're going to take on, because it's no longer emotion, it's STRUCTURE. Remember, you can't fool mother structure. That's why it's important to have a structured meal plan, a time of meditation and prayer, structured morning and evening routines, a set bedtime—yes even for adults. We need a structured one-day goal, seven-day goal, thirty-day goal, and beyond.

Submitting to structure has now taken all of our dreams, and not only made them bigger, but forced me to act accordingly. And that's why I can say it is adamant that you DREAM BIG, but you ACT BIGGER.

BONUS RESOURCE

Take immediate ACTION on what you LEARN! Get your free bonus resource, the **Conference Action Plan**, by visiting ChurchBoyToMillionaire.com

DREAMS TAKE ACTION

When we have DREAMS or DESIRES that are so BIG we're embarrassed to tell people around us, we're simply around the wrong people. It may require leaving the people who give us flack and getting around others who will encourage us. God did not put that DREAM inside of us to mess with our heads. It's there because it's time to start taking ACTIONS toward making it a reality.

CHAPTER TWENTY FOUR

BREAKING DOWN THE FOUR WALLS

I know this chapter will go against popular opinion—but I'm OK with that if it helps just one leader adjust, innovate, or stop living the status quo. However, what I'm about to say is already happening in many churches and private schools that are struggling to keep their doors open.

In the next five to ten years we will see more and more church buildings that were once packed sitting empty. This will happen to those who don't quickly innovate in how they go to where the people are at, rather than asking them to come to their building. I'm willing to guess that nearly 50 percent of church buildings today will be sitting empty. Also, within the next decade, we'll start seeing many empty private school buildings as well. And both will be followed by public schools going to online options shortly thereafter.

Yes, you are reading this right!!!

It's not a wish or a guarantee, and it hurts to say because I'm a church boy who's a product of the church and private education. It's just a sad—but most likely true—observation that times are changing. Some leaders will adjust and innovate, and others simply won't. Instead they'll choose to rest, stay old-school, and actually complain to their congregations about how the church needs to stay the church (building), not use social media, and not fall for the speakers taking their messages online. You know what that truly is? FEAR, and choosing not to evolve and grow. And guess what? It's holding people up.

The schools, churches, or organizations that will sadly be empty will be the ones with positional leaders, with leaders who don't immediately innovate and accept the changing times. Those that make it will start accepting more people, figure out a way to get their message out daily, learn to effectively educate and communicate with their audience, and develop a new audience—all while creating a community using new technology before they lose their people.

HOW TO STAY RELEVANT

People's lives look different now. Communication is different. Sure, people still love Jesus and value the church. It's just that what's going on in people's homes and lives is different for many, and we as leaders must be sensitive to that. Also, community is actively built online through video technology, and it's actually giving people a closer daily connection from all parts of the country, not just in their own town or area.

Those who desire to change, grow, and walk closer with God are always in the game, but not always in their seats on Sunday mornings. These people—and frankly, most people—desire something to fill their

cup daily. They need that quote and/or quick message to get them through the day. If leaders don't become that person or ministry their people can depend upon for frequent content that fills them up, they will go find it somewhere else. And sadly, they probably won't see them again.

Why is my online coaching business so successful, you ask? Well, I gather our group a few times per week through online video calls, we have private social media groups, and we are in daily community with each other, doing LIFE on platforms that we are are all on daily anyways.

Today is about BEING the church daily, even hourly, with a few friends or family members, versus just going to church for a once-a-week fill-up. Just to be clear, weekly church services are valued and needed, as long as the church or pastor also meets people throughout the week.

Pastoring, or leading anything, looks different today. If leaders only give one message from one platform one time per week on SUNDAYS, then they'll soon become irrelevant. Also, sales managers or leaders of great companies who simply rely on weekly conference calls won't get it done, either. It's just not enough in this ever-connected world. The ones connecting will grow and develop the fastest.

It's going to take creating content with an active Instagram, Facebook, or Twitter account using LIVE video. It means showing our lives (off the stage or platform), what we're reading, doing, listening to, and praying for. It means sharing #TwoMinuteMondays or #FiveMinuteFridays videos. It looks like constant posts and ENGAGEMENT while ADDING VALUE to your social account to actively pastor, coach, or mentor people. Even podcasting, or sharing more than Sunday messages, is an absolute must.

Those who do the above will most likely have full buildings and thriving churches. Sunday will be a bonus that's accelerated by what they already get a few times a week. Tithes and offerings will increase because people are being fed daily, and not just on the weekend.

My friends, as I write this, it is 2019. Simply asking people to come to us and giving them three to four ways to give will no longer get it done. Currency is exchanged as value for value. The truth is, if they're given three to four ways to give, they'd better be fed with content in three to four different ways. That is our duty as leaders.

JUDAH SMITH

I want to congratulate someone for whom I have much respect, even though I don't know him personally: Judah Smith, the former pastor of The City Church. I was recently on Instagram and saw him announce the launch of a new church—which is probably the most innovative church today. It's called Churchome and has locations in Washington state, California, and globally online! (Check it out at www.Churchome.org) He's literally started an online church powered by technology. It's a pretty cool setup.

YOUR ABILITY TO ADAPT DETERMINES YOUR IMPACT

———

Flexibility and the ability to quickly adapt determines how fast you will grow, impact the world, and whether or not people will want to work with you. Your ability to adapt and change in different environments, situations, and unforeseen changes is key—especially when things don't go your way. You must adapt quickly without losing your 💩. Your emotional well-being will determine your overall impact, earning power, and even the influence you have. Keep it together and always be growing in your emotional intelligence.

There's a hangout spot, a messaging experience, a worship experience, and even a lobby experience.

Congratulations, Judah, on being a forward-thinking pastor, not fighting tech, getting in our newsfeeds, and increasing your reach. You are now in all 50 states and the world, and not just a shared space.

By the way, pastor, if for some reason you're frustrated with Judah's approach, or the Steven Furticks, Carl Lentzs, and Joel Osteens of the world, why don't you stop being frustrated and join them? Why don't you do the same? This is how we will bring the Good News. We'll share it across the world by sharing our hearts, wins, and challenges with the people where they're at—and make an impact on humanity.

Now, you might be saying, "Doug, I get it, I want in. But where do I start?" Well my friend, I'm glad you asked . . . .

SOCIAL MEDIA JUMPSTART

Imagine if you could impact 100 people with your ideas, dispensing your knowledge and ideas about something you already know, and then quickly have them pay you for your advice, product, or service. How incredible would that be?

Now, imagine a year from right now, you're doing this with 1,000 people. A year later, you're impacting over 5,000. And within just a couple years, your product or service is impacting 10,000 or more people. You have become a respected person of influence in your field. Well, my friends, that is how it's done today—and this is exactly what I've done for the last seven years. And what I'm about to show you is exactly HOW I've done it.

We're going to call this a social media jumpstart. Because, as I've shared throughout the book, I know what it can do for your business if you get up on current tech, and then stay up. All I can say is buckle your seatbelt, and get ready to impact people's lives with your content, products, and services.

Like you heard me share in Chapter 14 about monetizing your unique ability, when you add massive value, you WILL increase your income. Remember, your unique ability is the essence of both what you love to do and are best at. It's the passion that fuels you and helps you contribute MASSIVE value to others. It's different for everyone because it describes what makes YOU who YOU are. It doesn't matter what your ability or profession is.

So, I'm going to share a few examples for multiple professions, because I know you are ready to get started. Now, before I give you your social media jumpstart, there is something you also need to understand about social media. I've told you how fast it's accelerating. The truth is, it will continue to speed up, which is also why you need to get on it now before it laps you. However, this information I'm about to share with you will very shortly be outdated. Not because it's not true today, but the rate of change may invalidate it tomorrow.

So apply it quickly, but never shy away from technology, or you will get left behind.

STEP ONE: GIVE VALUE SIX DAYS PER WEEK

Pastor: People want to see your life. They want to see a selfie of you doing sermon prep. They want to see you at your coffee shop. They want to see you working out. They want to hear a life tip or encouraging word when you're inspired. They want to hear how inspired you are for the weekend's message. They want advice on deepening their meditation and prayer time. They want to see what it looks like behind the baptismal 😌. Start highlighting the volunteers and taking pictures with them on Sundays, then post the pictures throughout the week and tag them.

Sidenote, pastor: Get ready, this will be meeting people where they're at. Be ready for Sunday attendance to start increasing.

Musician: I know nothing about music or singing, but I'm interested in learning. So, I need to know everything about your instrument. I need to know where you want to play and where you're going to play next. I need to see you practicing. I need to understand the process of songwriting. How could I start if I wanted to write a song? Is it fun? Is it easy? Are you teaching your kids to play? Snap a photo. I would love to see you playing your unique ability with the people you love most. I would love to see if you give lessons—show me a video of you giving lessons. The point is, bring me into your world. And chances are, soon enough, I'll be paying and respecting you for it.

Leaders: There are so many great books on leadership you have read. They're sitting on your bookshelf. Please start quoting those books and posting about them. Please help me understand the essential skills and mindsets of a leader today. I need to understand the mistakes you've made and how you've learned. I need to apply your lessons in my family, my church, and my organization. Help me understand the keys to becoming a person of influence. And soon enough, you'll be building leaders out of the huge number of followers you attract.

Nutrition or Personal Trainer: I need to see results, lots of results. Show me pictures of clients on your program. I would love to see photos of you training clients. What are some sample meal plans? How much water should I be drinking per day? Do you have any tips on emotional eating? What about stress eating? Do you have ideas on how to help my teenager eat healthier? What are some exercise routines that are easy to do from home?

Are we seeing the pattern, my friends? You can take your unique ability and add value to this world, and from there, monetize it and massively increase your influence.

STEP TWO: GET ON VIDEO

Here's the truth. If you're not on video in the next two years, you will soon be irrelevant, or at least at a serious disadvantage. So, hold that cell phone up in front of your face and push record. If people can LOOK into your eyes day after day, week after week, and hear your heart for what you do, how YOU can encourage them, or how your service can help them, you will have PURE TRUST and create relationships for LIFE. You can do this even in just two or three minutes. They will see you care about them, not the numbers, or just the money. Add VALUE to them at least a couple times a week. Become a dependendable source every day, and not just on Saturdays or Sundays.

You will cast so much VISION for people just by being on camera. I know you are scared. Truth is, we all are. I am scared every time I go live, but it does get easier and your confidence will build. AND it doesn't have to look perfect. People don't want your perfection, they want YOU from the HEART. Times are changing, my friends. Let's make the change with them.

Now, here are my best video and LIVE video tips to get you started and maximize connections:

1. **Make eye contact.** Avoid wearing sunglasses if possible, and make sure your eyes are fully visible. If it's bright out, find a different place to record. Remember, you are not trying to look cool, you are CONNECTING. Eyes build trust. No eyes, no trust.
2. **Look at the camera (green dot).** If you're LIVE, only read the comments when you are engaging. If you are sharing content, stop engaging and speak your points. It's distracting when you keep saying "Hello" or making funny comments if you are in the middle of a serious point. Plus, it takes you off course of your original message. However, even if you are speaking on a serious subject, at least be bright and light at the beginning before getting into it. Don't be too serious right out of the gate.
3. **Talk to one person.** Try your best not to say "you guys" or "hey everybody." Remember, if you talk to one person you will talk to everyone. But if you try to talk to EVERYONE, you will CONNECT with no one. Practice this and you will get better.
4. **Be clear on your topic and speak about that.** Have neither a bait-and-switch topic nor one that makes people guess what you

are going to talk about. If it's too vague, only your "followers" will watch. And your followers don't pay your bills (and most don't have a desire to grow or change). They camp out on social media all day doing nothing.

5. **Make it about them.** If your social media is more about you, a rant, or something you feel you need to get off your chest, then my suggestion is don't do it. Remember, if your greatest desire is to grow your biz and help others, then our job is to offer value that enhances others' lives. Don't use video as a video blog all the time. If you do, it can just attract dramatic people and it will be a waste of time for you.

6. **Be yourself.** Be YOU; connect authentically. Without authenticity, you cannot maximize your connections. Plus, people can tell, which means you won't build trust.

7. **Make the daily commitment to be consistent in your videos and posts.** It's repetition and consistency that will make this work. One video is cool, but people don't start taking you seriously until you start doing ten or more per month.

8. **Don't try to be a motivational speaker if you have not earned it.** Or if you don't have the influence built yet. Stick to content you are in the process of, that you're personally learning, and feel most passionate about. I have never said that to build an online business you must post positive quotes or do Facebook LIVE shots about random topics. However, if something is truly speaking to you and authentically coming from your heart, share it.

STEP THREE: FORGET THE HATERS

As you know, social media is its own unique beast. It's incredible, but I just want to prepare you, people tend to give their opinions freely—even when unwelcomed! But first of all, you will never be able to pay your bills with other people's opinions. My bank doesn't cash opinions, and I bet yours doesn't either 😄. So, just stay focused on the value you are adding. Second, regardless of whether or not you get weird comments or messages—you probably get at least ten positive comments and thank yous for each negative one. Third, fall in love with the unfollow, delete, or block button, and use whenever necessary 🚫.

STEP FOUR: GET OBSESSED

As I said before, social media is moving at lightning speed. It's time for you to start moving just as fast. If you're serious about this, I'm going to ask you to fully commit to learning social media, understanding the different platforms, and start taking massive action today.

Understand, this is not going to feel normal at first. And it shouldn't! You're disrupting a pattern in your life to create something abundant. This will take leveling up your frequency, consistency, and just ole-fashioned hard work. However, I'm adamant that you start this immediately.

DOUGISM #37

YOU'RE SCARING PEOPLE

Your growth scares people who don't want to change.

With social media, the longer you wait, the more you think about it, the more you over-analyze it, the more you will tend to procrastinate. Tomorrow comes, but the post never does. This is one of the biggest misses for those with big goals and dreams, who want massive churches, who want to build thriving businesses, or who even say they really wanna help people. However, these people are not on social platforms daily, utilizing a free service that won't always be free. It gives you instant access to the entire world.

Did you hear me say that? I said the entire world—in a moment's notice.

The hardest patterns to disrupt are our own. Stop thinking about it and making it all about you. Nobody's looking at that zit on your face anyways! Everyone needs to hear your wisdom and be encouraged. They need to know they're in it with someone else. Now go add value to people's lives and impact our communities and social circles. And let's build incredible organizations while we're at it.

START NOW

The truth is, there will come a day where we tell our grandkids about the time when social media was free! They won't believe it when they hear it. My friends, our chance to add massive value to people's lives is right in front of us. But it will not be this easy, this inexpensive, or this monetizable forever. Don't start "this year." Don't start "next month." Don't even start "next Monday."

Start now.

BONUS RESOURCE

Utilize SOCIAL MEDIA and CURRENT TECHNOLOGY to add value to people where they're at! Get your free bonus resource, the **Social Media Jumpstart**, by visiting ChurchBoyToMillionaire.com

RANDOM MESSAGE OF KINDNESS

One of my favorite things to do is step into someone else's world for thirty to sixty seconds and truly let them know I care. You know, I'll send a simple voice text or message, or instead of posting on their wall for their birthday like two-hundred other people, I'll send a private message with fifteen words letting them know they are valued. Or I'll take a little extra time commenting on their post letting them know THEY matter. Just by making meaningful connections, we can change someone's day while building incredible trust with them.

CHAPTER TWENTY FIVE

WHAT WE EAT IN PRIVATE, WE WEAR IN PUBLIC

For much of my high school and adult life, I was the one avoiding the camera. You know, the person that always lurks in the back of the group photo. Or the person told to angle the picture or selfie to get their most flattering side. Or the one who offers to take the photo every time. Well, that was me.

My wife can tell you how many events I dreaded going to, avoided going to, and tried to get out of last-minute if I could do it. I was so insecure that I had anxiety, because honestly, I would rather stay home and eat alone.

The physical weight and what it was doing to my psyche when I wasn't confronting it head on caused my head to spin in unhelpful directions. It spurred negative thoughts about myself that constantly reinforced insecurity. It even caused emotions that affected my personality and the way I interacted with my friends, coworkers, and the church community. I hated this about myself. I had spent many years on countless

diets, on running around the block, then going back inside and checking the scale to see if I lost weight.

Guys, I just didn't know how to create health for myself. I was an infomercial junky. I was not raised in a healthy home. I didn't understand nutrition. I was born at ten pounds, and eating became a self-defense mechanism. I felt bipolar, and was spinning out of control.

NO SUGARCOATING

I'm not going to sugarcoat this (pun intended), but this chapter will be hard for some of us. But for many leaders, it's time for a reality check. Do people take wildly unhealthy leaders seriously?

Leaders, pastors, business owners, and speakers: if your physical health is too far out of order, then many people will not take you seriously. It's that simple!

When health is out of alignment, it's obvious there is lack of self-discipline. Even if what you have to say is AMAZING!!! It's just that the message will not be received as effectively as it could be. No, these people are not judgmental. It's just the way our brains are wired. But I have a question for you: Do you want to be a transformational leader? Then be an example.

No need to be perfect, because I'm sure not. However, it's important to be on the path to wherever it is you're leading people in order to be taken seriously!

CAN YOU LOOK IN THE MIRROR?

It saddens me, but people don't wake up in the middle of the night and wonder how their hair color came to be. They're not thinking about getting their next pedicure. They're not wondering if their skin is hydrated. Instead, they're waking up in the middle of the night, going to the bathroom, and can't even bare to turn their heads at the mirror and see themselves naked. We've gotten to the point where we or some of us can't even be seen naked in front of our spouse because of the shame, even though they love us unconditionally.

What about intimacy with our spouses? Can we make love with the lights on? Let me tell you, Thea and I couldn't until about eight years ago. And let me tell ya, now it's frickin' awe-some 🍆. Thea did her part in getting healthy, but she needed me to step up. And as a leader, boss, and dad, I needed to accept personal responsibility. Even though I was born at ten pounds and modeled a diet to my kids of potato chips and sour cream for the movie snack, it became my fault if I didn't change.

Leaders, our teams are looking at us and STARVING for the real leaders to please stand up and show their self-discipline and commitment!

LISTEN TO YOUR BODY

Recently, a good friend of my father died unexpectedly from weight-related issues. You see, his father was extremely overweight, and always had been. And much of the family is also. I hadn't seen him in awhile until he posted photos on social media of the entire family gathered around the casket at the funeral home.

My jaw hit the floor. Here, a father was gone way too soon because of weight-related issues, leaving kids and many young grandchildren. It was blatantly obvious that the legacy this father left was one of love, family connections, strong faith, and even money. However, this father also left behind a generational beast that plagued this family.

Every single blood-related son and daughter was a minimum of one- to two-hundred pounds overweight. Please hear my heart; I'm not here to judge. But in my line of work, over the last eight years, I have seen way too many family members leave way too soon because of the legacy of poor physical health they inherited. Somebody chose NOT to be the family patriarch, confront the beast head on, and start contending for their health.

Remember, we don't change others, we change ourselves. It's what we live and model, not what we say. Our families will follow. I'm not here to toot my own horn, but lemme get toot-ey 📢, Thea and I recognized this in our family years ago.

We were poked fun at. Here Doug and Thea go again, on another diet. One family member even said, "Doug, you're good at starting. But I've never seen you finish what you start." While I'm glad I never quit trying, I never confronted my beasts.

ABOVE-AVERAGE DESIRE

Oh, I was an average boss, average leader, average volunteer, average husband, average dad. But one thing about me that was not average, I ALWAYS had an above-average desire to lose weight. As you read in Chapter 1, I had dark and depressing days. But there was always a fighter's spirit deep down within me trying to get out. Just as much as we're bringing heaven to earth, your body is trying to get into alignment with your spirit.

My friends, your bodies are fighting and crying out, saying to some: "You are strong spiritually," to others: "You are strong financially," to others: "You are strong in leadership and communication skills." But, my friends, your bodies are now crying out for alignment, saying they can't carry this weight much longer before we both pay a price.

Even if you're not going to do it for yourself, there are people in your life right now that need you healthy. They need you contending harder and more. Your kids need you. Your spouse needs you. Your organization needs you to step up and LEAD the way. Our excuses are getting old, not only to us but to the people who love us and need us.

I can authentically give this challenge because I'm nine years into this journey with you. I'm letting you know, I'm nowhere near perfect. But I'm still on the journey, still contending every single day. And I hope you will be, too.

THE 10 ZONES OF HEALTH

To help you start, I'll share what I call the "10 Zones of Health." Most are personal to me, but many will apply to where you are or may have been. Please understand also, you will move in and out of these zones, because they're moving based on our seasons, emotional cycles, and circumstances. It's also important to understand that one is not better, or worse, than another. These are just stages that most people go through or get stuck in. Remember, some people wear their struggle, others deal with it internally.

Here's how it works.

NEVER APOLOGIZE FOR YOUR GROWTH

———

I used to walk into a room and wonder if people liked me. Now I wonder if I like them. Be ROCK SOLID in who you are. Never apologize for the AUTHENTIC and REAL you. If you are growing and others are not, then oh well. Stay on the frequency of what you want most and step into it. I never apologize for where I am, or where I'm going. Either get on my frequency, or we don't hang much. Never waste your time trying to explain who you are, or what you are about, to people who are committed to misunderstanding you.

1 – 3 Denial and Avoidance

People in these zones can often feel stuck in blaming themselves with a lot self-pity, blaming others, or blaming their genes for their health problems. It can even be a sore subject with a spouse if brought up. Often, people in these zones find laughter at their own weight—or being the "big guy"—to be more comfortable, as it's an identity or safety zone.

4 – 6 Contending and Breakthrough

Zones 4 through 6 are where change starts to happen because at least they are trying to do something about it. BUT there is still some self-pity, blaming, and often secrecy around attempting to lose weight. However, people in these zones have potential to see positive improvements and momentum because they are now fighting for health even through setbacks.

7 – 10 Consistency and Desired Outcome

Everything starts to change in zones 7 through 10, because those here begin to realize their desired outcome! Unhealthy habits have now been identified and new habit-loops are forming. People in these zones understand themselves better, have fewer breakdowns, and are experiencing alignment with their spirits and bodies. Best of all, they are starting to live it and make the daily commitment to be consistent. It's important to understand health is not only a number on the scale. It's a mindset and daily commitment health.

10 Zones of Health

LINE OF **CHANGE**	LINE OF **BREAKTHROUGH**	**REALIZING DESIRED OUTCOME**
ZONES 1 - 3	ZONES 4 - 6	ZONES 7 - 10

ZONE 1: DENIAL!

- *In Zone 1 we say things like, "My health is my business, and it's affecting no one else but me."*
- *We are in denial and won't go to the doctor or step on the scale.*
- *We compensate with baggy, stretchy clothes.*
- *Often, we let personal hygiene slip and self-care stops being a priority.*
- *In this zone, we believe there's no real problem, and that we will always be this way, so we might as well stop trying to do anything about it.*

ZONE 2: BLAMING AND GIVING UP

- *People find themselves in Zone 2 when we believe our poor health isn't a big deal. Really, we have made peace with it.*
- *We say things like:*
  - *"This is the way I've always been. My family has always been big."*
  - *"I inherited these habits, it's not my fault."*
  - *"I'm big boned, this is just the way I am."*
  - *"I've just always liked being the 'big guy.'"*
  - *"My spouse wants me to stay big."*
- *In this zone, many even convince themselves that it's vanity to care.*

ZONE 3: CYNICISM, COVERING UP, LAUGHTER, AND JOKES

- *In Zone 3 we often use humor as a shield.*
- *We get the "fat joke" out before anyone else can—but it's often from a wound or continued childhood identity that keeps us seeing ourselves this way.*
- *We have developed the self-defense mechanism of hiding our own resentment towards healthy people, or we even make excuses for why we think some healthy people have it easier than we do.*
- *The truth is, secretly we want health, but we may still make fun of others pursuing a healthy weight so no one knows we care.*

The Line of Change

The Line of Change is the first mental barrier to break through on our journey to health.

ZONE 4: SECRETLY STARTING, AND TRYING, TO GET HEALTHY

- *In Zone 4 we are willing to try anything to lose weight and get healthy. Above everything, we want results!*
- *We try in private because we fear failure and embarrassment. And when things do get difficult, we start to wonder if maybe weight loss and health are impossible for us.*
- *We feel like this rollercoaster of weight will never end.*
- *We worry we have bad genes keeping us from either losing weight or keeping it off for good.*
- *We often diet for special events, occasions, or vacations, but quickly return back to old ways and weights within days.*

ZONE 5: THE "ANGRY" STAGE

- *In Zone 5 we find ourselves in an internal tug-of-war, like there are two devils sitting on our shoulders. We wonder which one's going to win each day—but growth and progress are taking place.*
- *Even with results, at random occasions we find ourselves binging and raiding the pantry or fridge. We feel out of control again, live with food hangovers, and start the whole angry process all over again. But, we don't give up.*
- *We overcome negative emotions, but are really pissed off at the process. We often throw in the towel for a weekend, but then get back to on Monday.*
- *We often eat or drink to excess in private, or find ourselves sneaking and hiding food.*

ZONE 6: QUESTIONING "WHY ME?"

- *When we are in Zone 6 we still hit the wall of frequent self-pity.*
- *We might still be asking ourselves:*
  - *"Why does it have to be like this?"*
  - *"Why has this always been my struggle?"*
  - *"Why is my flesh so weak?"*
- *In this zone, we even wish we could trade our struggles with weight for a different ones.*
- *It's our place of pain. But the question is, will we make it our place of reign? We are so close to breakthrough.*

The Line of Breakthrough

The Line of Breakthrough is where permanent change starts to happen.

ZONE 7: FORMING HEALTHY MIND AND HABIT LOOPS

- *Often, by the time we reach Zone 7, it's important we have made a DECISION! The decisions to be healthy, and not just lose weight. Health is a decision.*
- *We start to experience alignment in our body and our spirit. We see hope, often for the first time.*
- *We still deal with identity issues, body image issues, worth issues, and feelings that we "don't deserve to be healthy." These just takes time and consistency to break through.*
- *We better understand our triggers and change underlying structures to break unhealthy cycles.*

ZONE 8: CHOOSING HEALTH AND A NEW FUTURE

- *Zone 8 is where we take the power back by taking total personal responsibility of our health, our family's health, and reconfirm our decision. There is no going back.*
- *We understand that health is a choice and we cannot cheat it—we either choose our old life or the future we want.*
- *There are also no more secrets here. We bring our health into the light, showing and coaching others to do it also.*
- *In this zone, we elevate our frequency with healthier friends and relationships that ultimately help us create a healthier body.*

ZONE 9: TRANSFERRING HEALTH

- *In Zone 9 we understand that by getting healthy and modeling consistency, we are now transferring our health to the next generations.*
- *We contend and become chain breakers—for ourselves, families, and even our friends.*
- *We also understand health is a continued journey. It never stops, so we invite people into it by sharing our own stories. This keeps it in front for us for self-confirmation and provides hope to others.*
- *We are respected and become people of influence when we are consistent and have done all of this.*

ZONE 10: THE (CONTINUED) DAILY COMMITMENT TO BE CONSISTENT

- *When we are in Zone 10 we aren't perfect—we are just obsessed with moving forward.*
- *We stay consistent by always keeping our next goal in front of us.*
- *Because we live above the line and contend for our health, we are part of a community who live and operate on the same frequency.*

- *In this zone, we make the daily commitment to be consistent as we pursue the healthiest version of ourselves because we are our greatest asset.*

5 THINGS TO LOOK FOR IN A HEALTH PLAN

As part of growing through the 10 Zones of Health, many will look for a structured health plan. Over the years, I've tried many—for myself and in helping others. But here are the five most important things to look for in a successful health plan.

1. **Get an easy-to-follow lifestyle meal plan.** It must involve a structured eating plan, including: five to six small meals per day, lots of energy, and quick results.
2. **Find someone to coach you.** Find someone on social media or around you who is having results, or seems to be on their journey, and ask them if they have some ideas or tips and would be willing to coach you on your new health endeavor.
3. **Get your mind healthy, too.** Understand that your mind getting healthy is as important as your body getting healthy. Make sure your plan has a healthy mental component so you can unlearn bad habits, and create good ones.
4. **Find healthy community.** Get around other people, invite friends, invite family, but find or create a healthy, thriving community on the same journey as you. There are lots of social media groups to help you with this.
5. **Get moving.** When you are at a healthy weight, and it makes sense for you, implement healthy movement and exercise. Hire a personal trainer if accountability is what you need. Or, join group classes like a bootcamp, Orange Theory, or some other spin class in your area.

FINISH STRONG

My friends, I am the person I am today largely due to getting my health in order and confronting this beast head-on. When my PHYSICAL HEALTH got into ALIGNMENT, my SPIRIT came ALIVE. My girls deserved a healthy dad to model, show, play, and pray with them.

One of my favorite daily routines is with my daughter, Amaya. We get up and work out together. Not because she has to, but because she chooses to. She saw me consistently go to the same class for eight months, then I invited her. Now, she invites me. Baby Kate cannot wait to turn twelve. Why? Because she too wants to go and start working out with us.

She even jokes: "Papa, can you tell them I'm twelve so I can go work out with you?"

My family tree began to change eight years ago. Today it continues to change and I'm building a new legacy. Phoenix will never even know that his dad used to be so unhealthy because I started taking care of that before he was born. I'm still cleaning up a few habits I didn't get in front of before Amaya and Kate. But please give my family grace, we're a work in progress. As my friend Corey says in his amazing new book, we're just *Chasing Better*.

Choose YOU today. Choose your FAMILY today. They are depending on you to be the healthiest and best version of yourself. Test me on this if you want to—or better yet, test yourself. Start on the path to the healthiest you today.

BONUS RESOURCE

My friend, CONTEND for your HEALTH! Get your free bonus resource, **The 10 Zones of Health Worksheet**, by visiting ChurchBoyToMillionaire.com

THE ELEPHANT IN THE ROOM

———

Stop ignoring the elephant in the room. Let me tell you what your friends, family, and everyone who loves you won't say: *I feel like I'm losing you to food and poor health choices. It's not funny, nor can this be ignored anymore. Please make you and your health a priority. I love you.*

Sincerely,
Your son, daughter, spouse, friend, and everyone else who loves you and needs you healthy

GREATEST HITS

MISSIONAL ENTREPRENEUR

Are you where I was a few years ago? Are you tired of asking for blessings, handouts, and donations? Are you ready to live above the line and be the one writing the checks instead of asking for them?

It's time we step up and take complete POWER over our finances, businesses, marriages, and mistakes. We must confirm we are operating in our own UNIQUE ABILITY. We have begun to monetize our unique ability by adding VALUE in an area that we know and are FULFILLED in. And we are on our way to creating second and third revenue streams while confirming we are on our purpose, or going through a repurposing season, with clarity for the future.

We MUST create multiple streams of INCOME so we have multiple ways to give back. Because this is pivotal for what I'm going to invite you to next. It's time to become a MISSIONAL ENTREPRENEUR.

My friends, can you imagine the impact we can make in our families, communities, charities, churches, and the countries around the world when we take PERSONAL RESPONSIBILITY for our finances, the frequencies we're operating on, the friends we associate with, and the abundance mindset we are creating? We must raise our incomes so our standard of GIVING is constantly on the rise.

This is a completely new mindset, and will require pattern disruption as you step into your future self. I am seriously going to ask everyone reading this book to become a missional entrepreneur.

I didn't ask you your current financial situation. I'm talking about what you want to create and what type of impact and legacy you want to leave for your family and those you care about. A missional entrepreneur starts by making a DECISION.

My friend, I'm just gonna tell you—I love being a missional entrepreneur. It's given me so many ways to give back. I won't tell you all of them, but here are a couple examples just to give you a glimpse into your future when you've taken the oath ahead.

We were at church last summer and the youth had just come back from an incredible camp. We loved hearing the testimonies and stories. Then the youth pastor mentioned that even though the camp ended up $2,300 over budget, it was okay because they figured it out. They would raise the money themselves.

I loved the mindset behind it because, you see, a missional entrepreneur doesn't meet a need like that passively. He doesn't have to "pray" about it, or even ask God, or check his bank account. He bosses up and cuts the check. So I walked up to the youth pastor after service and said, "Here's a check. Don't worry, youth camp is covered." And I could honestly tell you many more opportunities I've been given to personally boss up. But I won't. Because all the details of giving don't need to be advertised on social media or in this book. Still, I wanted to share this example with you to invite you join in bossing up. I know some of you are going to hate this, but for the context of the book I'm going to share real numbers.

Remember where we started this: money is neutral. Yes, we all know it can do bad things. But now you fully understand money can impact, bless so many lives, and do more good when there is more of it.

SUCCESS ISN'T A CUSS WORD

Some people are uncomfortable with the word SUCCESS!!!

Recently, I was listening to an interview, and the person being interviewed actually told the audience to be careful about chasing SUCCESS because they might become addicted. Really?!

I'm not sure why, but I've found out that some people do fear SUCCESS. Some think it means being a person who only seeks fame and fortune. Others don't like it because they feel they don't deserve it. And some think if they become SUCCESSFUL, people will form bad opinions about them and they'll lose friends.

People are going to form their opinions whether you are successful or not. I realized a long time ago that people are going to talk about you, so you might as well give them something good to talk about!

I've also noticed that SUCCESSFUL people are frequently called "lucky". . . (yeah, lucky they aren't lazy). But you know why? Because they didn't quit or run away when things got painful . . . when all they wanted to do was take the easy way out . . . when they wanted to back off, throw in the towel, and listen to all the noise around them. Instead, they chose to stay consistent. So, I guess if that's what you call luck, then OK. So, yes, I get called lucky often. And those of you who stay true to your calling and passion, you will be called "lucky" . . . errrrr . . . I mean "successful" as well.

It's all how you measure the word SUCCESS. Many of you are successful parents or own a successful business. Many of you are successful lawyers, pastors, and caregivers. Others of you are successful at helping people lose weight. Others of you have growing and successful churches, and many of you are incredible business coaches. Need I go on?

Guys and gals, it's OK to be successful—and use the word. Go after it. Be successful and pursue all you do with 100 percent passion to succeed. Please don't avoid the word SUCCESS by trying to find a replacement word. Call it what IT IS!!! You are SUCCESSFUL because you have chosen to live a life of consistency instead of settling for a life of mediocrity.

It's OK to be what and who you are designed to be. Own your zone, stand up, rise up, celebrate together, BE SUCCESSFUL! Please give your all everyday. Now, should I say it again?! SUCCESS! Be it, live it, own it. Success, succeeding, successful . . . just in case someone tries to think I didn't cover all the words.

SUCCESS.

Remember, successful people are frequently called lucky because they didn't quit, give up, or throw in the towel when everyone else did.

JUST-ENOUGH SYNDROME

The most dangerous amount of money I have ever made was $5,000–$10,000 per month. It's the place I got stuck, and where I see more people stuck in life.

You see, that amount is usually enough to take the pressure off what was driving you to build, grow, expand, and better your family. It's the most dangerous because we stop doing what got us here! We stop improving our skills. We start backing off of social media. We fail to start as many conversations. We stop adding as much value as we used to. We stop putting in overtime. We stop setting goals. We start binging on Netflix again, and our drive and hustle slowly fades away until our income drops again. Then we get serious for a while, until things improve a little. Then we start the oscillating cycle over again, drifting back to a "safe" status quo.

Stop settling for just enough, even when things feel comfortable.

BOSS UP AND PICK UP THE CHECK

Have more dinners with people who fight over trying to pick up the check when it comes, instead of people who ask the waiter to take things off their bill. The conversation is much different. On the other side, if you are always on the receiving end of someone else picking up the check, you better at least be offering to pay.

You better not be sitting there with puppy-dog eyes or leaving to "go to the bathroom" when the check comes, then coming back to thank someone for the blessing. That's not a blessing, bro, that's called MIDDLE-CLASS PANHANDLING. It's a BROKE MINDSET and you are making a living off of someone else's generosity. I can tell you this, you won't get invited back very often if you are this guy. Better yet, why don't you boss up, take PERSONAL RESPONSIBILITY, and put yourself in a position to start picking up checks—or at least be able to honestly put up a fight for it.

LOVE SEEING OTHERS WIN

Pay close attention to the people who don't clap when you win. It's often the people in our inner circle like this who we need to be aware of. Can you say, "I LOVE seeing other people WIN. And win BIG."? Today, I can. But it took me a while and I had to come to an honest place of being OK with who I am.

We all go at different speeds, and we must realize LIFE is better when we're celebrating others!!!! LOVE seeing people WIN. LOVE seeing them have breakthrough in their marriage, health, finances, purity, accomplishments, jobs, ministries, lives, or whatever it is they do. Nothing excites me more than seeing my friends WIN.

A winning mindset celebrates others.

BROKE AND SKEPTICAL

I was the biggest SKEPTIC for so many years of anything that was not "traditional" business. I was also broke with big dreams that got smaller and seemed further away as the years progressed. I was spending less time seeing my kids grow up, missing key events, and felt like I was saying no to them more than I was saying yes. I wanted to give more but never had the money to do more than tithe. TRUTH was, I was OWNED by the system that keeps good people living just below or above average.

When skepticism controls the heart it robs us from the expansion, growth, and opportunity that is often exactly the thing we are looking and praying for. Often it's what we learn after we "know" everything that makes the difference.

Sometimes we think what we are supposed to be doing, or our opinion of something, is an idea or assumption that someone (often an uneducated mom, dad, or friend) gave to us. We need to reject these lies.

Remember BROKE and SKEPTICAL is a bad combination.

I encourage you to expand your thinking, understand that you can make hundreds of thousands of dollars from your cell phone using the exact device you are scrolling Facebook on right now and love what you are doing, feel good about what you are doing, and take full control of your time.

If you feel like you don't control your time, you can't be where you want, your income is capped, or maybe you're even lacking purpose, then I encourage you to be open to new ways of making income. Remember this: observe the masses and "normal people" and do the exact opposite. Weird people do BIG things, are willing to break up with average, and choose a life that doesn't make sense to everybody else but makes sense to you and your current needs.

LET GO OF GRUDGES

Sometimes, a beast we need to confront can be a grudge or unforgiveness. I let go of my last grudge approximately five years ago, even though the other person still has not accepted any responsibility. It has been so freeing. Regardless of who was right or wrong, I realized it was hurting me more than them. My heart has been able to heal so much since then. I have never been or felt so free in my entire LIFE since letting go of that grudge.

ACTUALLY NO, THIS BOOK WASN'T ABOUT YOU. BUT IF THE SHOE FITS, FEEL FREE TO LACE UP A CHAPTER AND WEAR IT!

●

WHAT DO YOU SEE?

What do you see? Some of you see a black dot. I see a ton of white space. Imagine that black dot represents a certain situation in your life. Maybe it's your marriage, maybe it's your financial situation, maybe it's your income, maybe it's not getting that bonus, maybe it's blaming your last church, maybe it's how you grew up, maybe it's a family member, maybe it's even someone who hurt you.

Here is the problem, on the page, I only see white space. I guess there is a little tiny black dot, but I'm dead serious, I only see white. You know, this is the difference between how you see your problems and how I see them—or even how I see my own. They are your black dots and they're holding you up from FREEDOM and massive BREAKTHROUGH.

It's time we let those black-dot situations go. They're robbing you of moving on. Maybe it's just forgiving someone in your heart. Maybe it's time for you to stop being walked on, or time to put your resume out and actually get serious about your career. Maybe you should start a side hustle. The point is, step into the life of white-space freedom and experience joy, abundance, and breakthrough results.

TAKE MEASURABLE ACTION

For those of you that believe 100 percent of what happens to you, or for you, is up to God's will, have you ever tried putting measurable ACTION behind your WISH 🌿, HOPE ⭐, or PRAYER 🙏? Do it. Then watch what happens—or what GOD does. Good things and massive results will start to take place. Personally, I choose to PRAY like it depends on God but WORK like it depends on me. I no longer question this recipe. It works!

KICK FEAR IN THE FACE

Do you realize we have made-up stories in our heads that keep us from BREAKTHROUGH and getting what we really want? These stories we tell ourselves usually shield us from the hurt of what would happen if we tried, set a goal, made an exit strategy, or planned and things didn't work out. Get brutally HONEST with yourself and examine what B.S. stories YOU have chosen to believe and made up in your head. Fear or Faith—we can't see either one, so why not put pen to paper on the fear. Then do something about it and KICK FEAR IN THE FACE.

DON'T HOLD BACK

When we have a business, a message, a service, a tool, an idea, or something in our hands that we know others need and find value in, it is our DUTY to share it. I can't tell you how many times I feel like I have something I needed to say, but I held off. I didn't share it because of the fear of what people will think of me, or what they might say.

Let me share a little secret: People are not thinking of us. They are thinking of themselves, and they need LIFE breathed into them. What we have in our hands needs to be shared with more people. My encouragement is for us to start promoting ourselves and our messages. Even if it's just for one person—they need to hear our message. Doing this may change a LIFE!

PEOPLE BE LIKE, "DOUG, YOU CHANGED!" YEAH... YOU THINK I WORK THIS HARD TO STAY THE SAME!?

@THEREALDOUGWOOD

FAITH MOVES MOUNTAINS, DOUBT CREATES THEM

Your faith can move mountains, but your doubt can create them. Squash your doubt with ACTION then tell me how much your FAITH increases! Now pick up the phone and text or call someone you're scared to. Do it! They need your call as much as you need to make it. Don't work eight hours for a company, then go home and not work on your own goals.

You're not tired, you're uninspired.

We have the tendency of giving the best of ourselves, and our efforts, building someone else's company or dreams. At some point we need to STOP, challenge our own thoughts, desires and, goals, and CHOOSE to start building them. Usually, it begins to happen after hours of grinding, working when no one can see you. Also, turn off that stupid TV. It's killing you and your future. My friends, don't live last year over again.

Unless, of course, you just finished your best year ever. Then duplicate your SUCCESS and continue to EXECUTE!!

90-MINUTE GROWTH HACK

The first ninety minutes of your day belong to YOU, your DREAMS, and your VISION for life. I encourage you to spend time nurturing *yourself* and getting *yourself* right before serving everyone else. Remember the people you love—*and who love you*—are the ones who most deserve you at your best.

Some great things to do first are: pray, read, develop yourself, work out, write down your goals, and get clarity on what you will accomplish that day. After that, you can start checking notifications, emails, and texts.

The best way to starve procrastination is to pack your calendar so tight that it keeps you in constant action. It will also starve moods and feelings that send us into depression. Protect yourself and energy! Now, stop *reading* the news feeds and start *making* them.

WHAT'S THE RISK, WHAT'S THE COST?

What's the RISK? What's the COST? What's the risk if you take the next step? What is the risk if you don't? Consider ALL COSTS and set a timeline of no more than a few days to PRAY for PEACE and CLARITY. Then, make a decision and take ACTION. For most people, NOT moving forward is the greatest risk. So jump, leave, execute, and take that next step, even though it's uncomfortable.

Inaction happens only because FEAR has a slimy way of crippling us into procrastination or to keep us saying, "I need to pray about it," long after we already have a clear answer right in front of us. Other times, we play the God Card, to delay obedience or truth!

The answer to HOW is YES.

IF YOU DO, OR IF YOU DON'T

There is a risk and a price to pay for every choice. Just make sure as you are getting clarity, you consider both sides. Staying where you are, or being "comfortable" and letting the day, the week, the month repeat itself, usually only leads to depression and anxiety.

No one is coming to bail us out.

If you're not truly happy and content, then don't join three fantasy football leagues, watch four series on Netflix simultaneously, smoke and drink five nights a week, and then complain and moan about your financial situation. The government doesn't care about us. Most of our families are financially ignorant. They live with a poverty mindset and are in debt up to their eyeballs. At the same time, they tell us to not chase success or money because "it's not important." Most schools and universities are thirty years behind the times, preparing us for a robotic workforce that's now irrelevant. No one is coming to educate, enrich, or empower us to achieve freedom in our lives. It's our responsibility

Become aware of and awake to the price of staying where you are.

IS YOUR OFFLINE GAME STRONGER THAN YOUR ONLINE GAME?

Always make sure your OFFLINE game is stronger than your ONLINE game. If it's not, you will feel incongruent and fake. You'll feel pressure to make up stuff to post, and even start to copy and paste stuff making it appear to be our own. Very soon, others will start to notice it.

Always LIVE what you post! If you can't think of anything real, it's OK to have an off day or two. Take some time to work on yourself. You will find authentic clarity, and in no time, your fingers will be dancing.

SELF-AWARE

To become an "emotionally conscious" person or leader means knowing how you tend to react under pressure, stress, or when you have setbacks. I will be honest, I still stress eat in these situations sometimes. I also have the tendency to withdraw or isolate myself. I'm still working on these habits. But the important part is, I'm aware and conscious of them. Therefore, I can grow and develop in them.

A great way to identify areas in which we are "emotionally unconscious" is to ask someone who loves you unconditionally and knows you well: "How do I react when . . . ?" Ask them the question for the specific area in which you want to gain self-awareness. Then listen! Do not argue with their answer. If you do, they will never tell you the truth again—and then you are really screwed ☺. Simply accept their feedback, say thank you, consider it, and work on becoming more self-aware.

AM I COACHABLE?

Recently, I asked three great leaders in my company if I could individually coach them on something I noticed that would help them improve, grow, become a better leader, and a person with more influence.

WE MUST MAKE THE
DAILY COMMITMENT
TO BE CONSISTENT.

@THEREALDOUGWOOD

All three of them answered the same: "YES!!! PLEASE!!!"

I coached them on just a few minor tweaks that I'm sure were hard to swallow. However, the response from each was: "THANK YOU," "OMG I had no idea," "Thank you for telling me, as I want to improve."

My friends, success leaves clues. These are amazing leaders and they are still 100 percent COACHABLE. Instead of an ego, they have a desire for growth over being right. This means they never let themselves get in the way. We all have blind spots. So make sure you have someone who cares about you enough to show them to you. But leaders, remember, always ask permission. Some are not ready for input and don't want to hear it.

My biggest question is, are YOU open? Because if I would get one ounce of push back, or feel defensiveness, I would have stopped and most likely never given someone like this advice again unless they begged for it.

Most leaders only coach the COACHABLE. How coachable are you?

KEEPING IT REAL ON SOCIAL MEDIA

Will the REAL you please post 😊?

People want to know the CHALLENGES you are overcoming. Then, they want to know HOW you overcame them. You know, messy-hair-don't-care days. They want to see the side of you that your family and friends get to see everyday. That's what we all want. We don't want your filter, your dream life, or your perfect relationship (which doesn't exist).

For example, I'm working so hard right now on this book in a hotel room in Los Angeles. I have my photo shoot just two weeks from today. I don't feel ready, but I'm doing the work. It was incredibly hard to say no to the adult beverages and appetizers last night at dinner with friends. I had a few extra bits of food that weren't part of my program. But I said no to dessert.

I'm a work in progress. I'm learning to not beat myself up or sabotage my health after an intense week, or even while I'm traveling.

It's not easy. I'm not perfect. I'm me.

When you share this side of yourself, your friends will actually CON-NECT and identify with you, love you through the process, and RESPECT you even more. If there are those who judge or can't handle it, delete them from your life—no time for fake people. Know your worth and don't take less.

GET OFF YOUR SPOUSE'S @$$

Thea and I have chosen to have a relationship without gender roles. After our first seven challenging years of marriage, we got clear on our common goal and stopped keeping score! We established a very CLEAR VISION for us and our family. It always trumps anything else and remains the focus.

Now, we both cook and take turns running the kids around. We're both hustlers, we both pray, we both pay, we both contribute. We both call each other out with respect, knowing that only the other's best interest is at heart. We are independent of one another.

The point is, it works for us. But each marriage or relationship has its own dance. The main thing that helped us dance to the same beat is establishing our big goal and non-negotiables together. Because we stay focused on them, small things don't creep in as easily. Anytime we feel like a conversation starts drifting below the line into blame, shame, finger-pointing, or even doing something distracting, we go back to the non-negotiables to refocus.

My challenge to you is get off your spouse's @$$! Support and amplify what they do well, find a common goal, and stop picking apart the small stuff. Our spouses need a safe place and a shoulder to cry on. They need to be encouraged for the things they are doing well. Let's make sure we are filling their cups.

Trust me, this is something I'm still working on. And I'm by no means perfect. But remember, WE ARE BETTER TOGETHER with our spouse.

OPINIONS DON'T PAY MORTGAGES

If there are people in your life giving you opinions you didn't ask for, or the classic, "Just wanted to give you a heads up of what other people are saying about you" (not them of course... 😄), then I suggest you evaluate their true intent. Ask yourself why you value their input in your life. Do you want their life? Do they live with an ABUNDANCE MINDSET, did they quit on their DREAM, or have they just never done what you are about to do? Perhaps God didn't give them your DREAM.

So, the next time someone gives you an unwelcome opinion about your life, ask them which one of your bills they'll be paying this month? Better yet, ask them to cover your mortgage and see how they respond.

EMBRACING CHANGE

We all love change, until things actually change! Learn to embrace change. If you really think things will stay the same as they are now, let me be your change whisperer: CHANGE IS COMING. The question is whether it will be on your terms or someone else's. Keep your growth and creative game so strong, and on your terms, that you embrace it and actually crave change. Because you know BREAKTHROUGH happens on the other side.

If you are in a funk, it's time for a change. If your job is too easy, boring, or no longer challenges you, it's probably time for a change. If your marriage is in a funk, it's time to change it up. Go see a marriage coach, get away for the weekend together—don't check out and quit. If your ministry is not growing, ARE YOU? Either GROW YOURSELF, or the things around you will grow without you. Remember, nothing ever stays the same. We are either moving forward or moving backward.

ALWAYS SHOW UP

It's time to get to know the author 😌.

So, I will just come right out and say it, getting a vasectomy was the most painful day of my life 😊. (Men who haven't had the procedure, I don't mean to scare you.) I finally decided to pull the trigger to get my well-overdue "man surgery" to confirm Phoenix is my last child 😵.

I went in to get my vasectomy and prepared just like I was told to—other than "cleansing" all of the exposed areas that require deep sanitation for this type of procedure 😊. Then, while laying on the hospital bed, the twenty-four year old female nurse told me, "Just relax."

Ha ha, yeah, you try relaxing! I was covered in nothing but a hospital gown with a hole cut out exposing me and all my thirty-nine year old glory 😊. The doctor proceeded, and other than some light pressure, all was good just twenty minutes later.

After the procedure—which went fine (I think 😛)—the doctor told me to get up, take off my gown, and get dressed. Then he would be back in a few minutes to discuss everything before leaving the office. However, while getting dressed I passed out cold and fell, hitting my head hard on the surgery table and cutting my face open.

Then, after what felt like an hour (but was most likely only ten minutes) later, I awoke to some nurses and very bright lights. The doctor was saying my name over and over again, asking me if I was OK. As I slowly regained consciousness, I realized I was lying on the floor buck naked 😵, humiliated 😵, and in a large pool of blood. Worse, I had peed all over myself while passed out because of a "numb southern region" that had just been operated on (if you know what I mean) 💩.

I guess I passed out from getting up too quickly. And my face hit the metal table that holds all the tools for procedures, cutting the side of my head wide open. Thankfully, my amazing wife and son were called in and were there to help me get dressed and cleaned up.

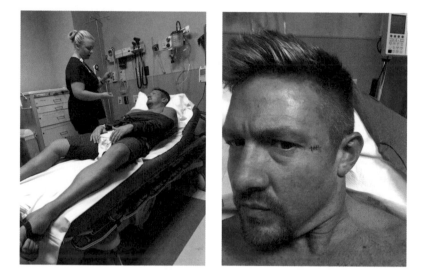

So, I asked the doctor to stitch up my face. And this is where it gets real. He said, "Uh, my sutures are made for men's balls, not your face."

Then I was like, "What? You're a doc, and you just stitched the most sensitive part of my body. But you can't do the side of my face?"

OK, so there we go, off to the ER for my second operation of the day 😔. Picture this: I'm holding ice on my entire southern "man area" and also a towel over my head with ice to try to stop the blood as I waddle myself into the ER to get my face stitched up. The best part of the story was that everyone in the ER wanted to know what happened to me.

Truthfully, they all thought Thea kicked me in the 🏐's and also knocked me out—because they evidently see a lot of that there 😱. We all chuckled at the story as they stitched me up. Truth be told, we all had a good laugh.

So, I had a black eye from hitting my head, and the stitches stayed in for a few days. But guess what? I had a video conference coaching call planned for the same day—and I didn't cancel.

Oh, I could have, and they would have understood. But professionals don't cancel for any reason, regardless of life's circumstances. The great news is, there's a scar on the side of my face near my eye to remind me of this oh so wonderful day, and of the importance of always showing up, whether I feel like it or not.

IT MIGHT LOOK DIFFERENT 😨😟😰

Understand that how you end up fulfilling your PURPOSE, DREAM or VISION might look different from how you originally thought it would or how it started.

The sooner you come to grips with this the quicker INTERNAL PEACE and BREAKTHROUGH can happen. Often IDENTITY or our own preconceived notions can get in the way of what God might be trying to do through us.

Personal Example: For two years I resented being a health coach as my own health was always a place of personal pain. I thought there was no way God could use me to help others in an area I had so much baggage in.

The truth was, my Identity was holding me up from being open as I told myself I'm a salesman, Furniture guy, and I'm not good with people and there is no way I could become a coach. I was soooooo WRONG!!!

Lies, lies, lies is what they were and also a huge amount of ego and pride as I was not open at the time to a new way of business that really

BE PREPARED. ANYTIME YOU START TO GROW, MOVE, OR DISRUPT THE STATUS QUO, THERE WILL BE MAJOR PUSH BACK FROM CERTAIN PEOPLE CLOSEST TO YOU. AT THAT POINT, YOU HAVE TO HOLD FIRM TO YOUR DECISION TO GROW.

didn't impact that many lives other than the few employees I was honored to give a job to.

When my furniture business was failing and the doors just kept closing no matter what I did to help it I said, "Alright God . . . Do you have a different path for me? Because this feels like a fight and coaching seems so easy and I'm honestly not even trying that hard."

What happened was I had become more open to my path being more non-traditional, and things began to explode and pieces fell into place.

The hardest thing was letting go of my pride, and questioning what was it all for?"

After that, I actually discovered my PURPOSE is to help average people become GREAT. God could take my biggest place of pain (my health) and make it his place of reign in my life and thousands of others.

I encourage YOU to be more OPEN and not fight the resistance of the internal tug.

God might be tugging at your heart in a NEW WAY for a NEW SEASON of what's ahead. He will lead you well if YOU stay open and truly keep it about HIS PURPOSE and YOUR PURPOSE coming together.

However I will tell you first hand that's a hard prayer to pray. Just be prepared for massive breakthrough that will leave you questioning the HOW. As for the WHY and the PURPOSE—those will be AMAZING for you, your family, and the people you will impact.

"BE CAREFUL DON'T CHASE MONEY 👻"

Uhhhh OK, would you rather keep chasing debt and depression? 🧟 Because that wasn't working out real well for me.

My friends, you should always seek PROFIT with PURPOSE! Stop repeating stupid things your parents said growing up. Anyone who says don't chase money is broke—doesn't have any. Stop listening to your broke friends' advice.

TRUE LEADERS GO OUT OF THEIR WAY

A true LEADER stays up late or does whatever is necessary to help others WIN and reach their goals, long after they have reached their own goals. True Leaders reach out and help others FINISH STRONG!!!! I don't care what industry you are in. If you are in the industry of partnering with people, and helping others WIN, then you do whatever it takes—inconvenience and late nights, if necessary.

QUIT ACTING BROKE

Quit acting like you are always broke. If you are, it's your mindset about money that's keeping you there. When the bill comes for dinner, and drinks, boss up and take pride in picking up the check for others once in a while. Build some pride in your self to refill your abundance tank.

PROFIT WITH PURPOSE

Always ensure you are living, working, and being 100 percent fulfilled where PURPOSE calls you to be, not just where a job or income calls you to be. Income without purpose is fine for a while but quickly causes confusion, mild-depression, and a feeling of being trapped or fearful to make the next move. Always have PROFIT with PURPOSE.

A MILLIONAIRE'S TIMELINE

1978 — Born in Banks, Oregon at 10½ pounds (God bless my Mom) with a bag of potato chips in my hand. I would be referred to as "Husky" for the next 20 years.

1989 — Held back in third grade. Had to stay inside during recess for speech therapy at Banks Christian Academy. Made fun of for missing recess and being unable to annunciate R's or S's. On a positive note, the ladies loved it.

1990 — Became a Christ follower! Continue following Jesus to this day.

1991 — This little Christ follower becomes the class clown and almost kicked out of his Christian school.

1992–1996 — Spent some of my greatest years playing varsity golf and football in high school, actively involved in my church youth group, spending amazing summers at camp, and working in my Dad's furniture business.

1997 — Graduated high school at nineteen with a C- average. Settled into a comfortable job at a pizzeria instead of going to community college. God intervened, disrupted my easy summer, and I reluctantly attended Master's Commission in Phoenix, Arizona, which would later change my life.

1999 — Met my future wife, Thea. We became fast friends, and then even more when my Mom invited her on a family houseboating trip. Sparks flew, emotions ran high ☺, and we started dating long-distance.

2000 — Left Master's Commission, married Thea, and started my first furniture business with my Dad's help at twenty-one years old.

2003 — The worst year of our marriage. We prayed, contended, and almost quit—so glad we didn't.

2004 — Oldest daughter, Amaya, was born. Bought our first house on the weekend of my birthday for $178,000, and it required no money down 😬. Speaking of down, my furniture business began its downward spiral.

2007 — A very big, ugly, blurry year. Second daughter, Katelyn, is born. My mom (Jeanette) is diagnosed with cancer and undergoes an intense stem-cell transplant. My business was doing so poorly I had to leave Thea in labor while I bid a job at a nearby office complex. I barely returned in time for Baby Kate's birth. My beasts ran wild, and frankly, I was looking for an escape plan. Creditors calling constantly. Vendors unwilling to ship product because of back money owed. Broke with $220,000 in unsecured debt and a building lease of $17,000 per month with 2 ½ years remaining and a personal guarantee with my name on it. The darkest year of my life.

2008 — Started store closing and liquidation sale of my furniture company in attempt to pay off debt. This would last six months. Continued paying off debt and making right on past debt while selling stuff on the internet and through garage sales to fulfill my commitment to others and myself.

2010 — My life finally begins to change, because I finally begin to change. Thea begins a coaching business and helps me lose 65 pounds of fat and what felt like a thousand pounds of shame.

2012 — Joined Thea's coaching business to share my success with anyone who will listen. Started the process of helping thousands of people change their bodies, minds, spirits, AND income. We start making massive changes, move into a large house, and are able to help my mother after she and my father divorce, as well as my sister, who was going through difficulties of her own. This was a hard season, but we said yes to opportunities, and breakthrough started to happen. Adopted a millionaire mindset and started living and acting out of abundance.

2012–2016 — Helped coach people all over the country to transform their lives, their health, and assist them to discover their purposes. Made wise financial investments, operated in our unique ability, utilized technology and social media to add value and make impact and income.

2014 — Moved from Tigard, Oregon to Scottsdale, Arizona, Needed a pattern disruption, a time to grow again and step out into uncharted waters. Plus needed more sunshine. We were finally in a place where we, and God, wanted us to be, and not just where income told us we could be.

2016 💰 — Continued the millionaire mindset and very soon would become actual millionaires by the world's standards 🎉. Purchased our dream property and home in North Scottsdale that would become a place of growth, refuge, abundance, and creativity, now called Breakthrough Acres where we host gatherings, do strategic coaching, have retreats, and raise our children. After much prayer and contending for many years by Thea, Phoenix is born and we welcome our first son.

2018 — Co-Founded Valor Global Online, an innovative school bringing synergy to students and their families worldwide. Coaching and living our lives to help others pursue profit with purpose. Traveled the world to Israel, UK, and all throughout Europe, Singapore, Bali, Dominican Republic and spent almost three out of twelve months overseas.

2019 — Wrote this book over the course of four intense days to help you change your life, health, family, organization, and income forever. Living my mission to help average people with above average desires become missional millionaires, find freedom, and change the freaking world. I imagine our entrepreneur family on a massive tour of the United States, speaking and sharing this message with thousands.

INTEGRATED LIFE

Just a family being intentional about helping others.

Hanging out with some of our very best friends, Mike & Sumer, at a New Kids On The Block concert.

Dad and his girls hitting up the range.

When Dan Valentine and I take our girls out for a double father-daughter date.

Playing my favorite golf course, Brandon Dunes.

I have a love for Nascar. But only when I have a HOT PASS.

For those about to rock, we salute you.

One of my favorite pictures of Amaya and Kate.

*Just a dad and his boy
dressed for success.*

*We love our country
and our freedom.*

*When you get your hands on
the famous Dr. A Sundance
jacket, you snap a picture* 😊

Watch out world... Amaya Rose is coming for you.

Just know they are
watching EVERYTHING we do.

A Jackson Hole Christmas.

The day my $17,000 per month lease ended
and I wasn't bankrupt. Locking the door after 11
years, for the final time, at my furniture store.

It's always a good time with the MANN family.

Boy getting baptized in Seahawk football.

Putting in a green and sand traps at Breakthrough Acres. Phoenix thinks it's his own sand pit.

Just a couple of kids with a dream to help others.

A walk down memory lane. The house where I grew up, in Forest Grove, Oregon.

Always be coachable.

A brotherhood of men on the same path and journey in life.

Thea enjoying the moment, and me rushing too much.

Our family and dear friends, the Oltean family.

Everyone should play Pebble Beach at least once in their life.

Celebrating Grandpa's 80th birthday as a family.

When you go on a cruise with your best friends for your 40th birthday.

Sometimes you find those people you can change the world with.

Friends that feel like family.

Well hello, chunky honeymoon...

No caption needed 😊

Just a husky kid ready for some baseball.

It was pure love in the summer of 1999.

When Phoenix is done with photos he flips us the bird.

Phoenix's first Halloween.

Family that changes the world together.

Great time with great friends.

Great friends hanging out at Sundance.

*My sister and the most loyal
person you will ever meet.*

What Breakthrough Acres is all about: Community.

ABOUT THE AUTHOR

Doug and Thea Wood are entrepreneurs who run a multi-million dollar independent coaching business. Over the last nine years, they have helped over 300,000 people improve their lives. They've dedicated their lives to helping average people (just like them) with above average desires to live and become their best selves.

They imagine a world where people live and express the riches within, rather than purely pursue the riches without. Doug and Thea's authentic and relatable communication style creates instant connections with anyone who desires more for their life.

They are in demand speakers, co-founders of Valor Global Online, an innovative school bringing synergy to students and their families world-wide, and the founders of Aradaya Media and Publishing.

They have also been called the entrepreneur family, as their three children, Amaya (14), Katelyn (11), and Phoenix (2), are also writing books, speaking, starting businesses of their own, and fully embracing their family's legacy. Most importantly, the Wood family has chosen to live life differently, set apart from average. When they're not travelling the world, they live in Scottsdale, Arizona at their property, Breakthrough Acres.

You can follow Doug and Thea at:

◎ *@TheRealDougWood*
f *@TheRealDougWood*

◎ *@KickFearInTheFace*
f *@KickFearInTheFace*

www.TheRealDougWood.com
www.ChurchBoyToMillionaire.com
www.KickFearInTheFace.com